More Praise for

SHAPING A LIFE OF SIGNIFICANCE FOR RETIREMENT

I wish this excellent overview of retirement had been available when I first "retired." I found very meaningful their conviction that in retirement we need not create a new self "but be who we really are in a fuller and more complete way." This book will be an invaluable resource to boomers on the cusp of retirement who seek meaning in their retirement years beyond the tedium of a carefree existence.

—Richard L. Morgan
Author of *Beyond the Rocking Chair: God's Call at Retirement*

As a financial planner whose practice consists primarily of working with retirees, I am keenly aware of the need for education and support regarding the nonfinancial aspects of retirement. *Shaping a Life of Significance for Retirement* will be a great asset for those in my field who incorporate holistic life planning into their practices. It offers a candid look at the problems, challenges, and joys that can be anticipated as we age. I think this book is a must-read for anyone who ever plans to retire!

—Donna L. Jordan, CFP®, CLU, AIF®

Shaping a Life of Significance for Retirement is not a book about financing retirement or managing relocation, nor is it a self-help volume. Rather it invites reflection on the elements and possibilities involved in a distinctly new stage of life: retirement. The authors discuss such important issues as developing relationships with family and friends, old and new; intellectual growth and service to others; perspectives for determining new goals for one's life and marriage; and dealing with the various problems of aging. It is a book about faith and values addressed to a growing and diverse audience.

—Bruce Rigdon
President Emeritus of Ecumenical Theological Seminary, Detroit

Without undue drama, the "work" of retirement is embodied in the stories of real people in this book. These representative experiences of men and women in this phase of their lives significantly contribute to the fullness of their lifelong journeys.

—Joan Stoffel, OSF

SHAPING A LIFE OF
SIGNIFICANCE
FOR RETIREMENT

R. Jack Hansen
and
Jerry P. Haas

UPPER ROOM BOOKS®
NASHVILLE

LIBRARY OF CONGRESS CATALOGING-IN-PUBLICATION DATA

Hansen, R. Jack.
  Shaping a life of significance for retirement / R. Jack Hansen and Jerry P. Haas.
    p. cm.
  ISBN 978-0-8358-1025-8
  1. Retirees—Religious life. 2. Retirement—Religious aspects—Christianity. 3. Aging—Religious aspects—Christianity. I. Haas, Jerry P. II. Title
  BV4596.R47H36 2009
  248.8'5–dc22

                                                        2009045126

CONTENTS

FOREWORD

WHAT IS IT LIKE to retire? What are the biggest challenges? What are the surprises and possibilities? What will it be like for *me*?

When we started examining the personal dimensions of the transition from full-time work to part-time work or full retirement, we anticipated finding a lot of experts who could help us answer these questions. We discovered instead that retirement experts mainly advise about finances and health but have little understanding of the more personal transitions that occur in relationships, self-image, and sense of personal significance. The few retirement advisers who have written about the personal issues tend to draw insights primarily from their own experiences rather than from a broader, representative population. Our goal instead was to listen to what retirees themselves said about the personal dimensions of retirement and then offer their wisdom, sometimes in their own words but more often as common themes and experiences, to others. Readers of this book may listen in as retirees reflect on their own lives.

This book is more about the retirees interviewed than about the authors. We do want to share a few things about ourselves, however, and our motivation for doing this work.

Jack has an engineering research background and moved from full-time to part-time work three years ago. As he and his wife, Pat, entered the early stages of this transition, they found themselves confronting challenges they had not previously considered. For example, they were offered the opportunity to teach abroad for two years, a possibility that forced them to think deeply about what was important to them in retirement. They realized that investing in the lives of grandchildren was a higher priority in these years, so they turned down the overseas offer. They also needed to decide whether to relocate in retirement. They moved to a new community, in part because of their priority on grandchildren, but also because a hurricane had displaced them from their home. Once in the new community, they had to come to grips with how to spend more time together, build a new network of friends, and invest their time in worthwhile pursuits.

This major life transition took place in the two years that Jack participated in the two-year Academy for Spiritual Formation, an intensive program in Christian spirituality for both lay and clergy. During the second year of the program, participants complete a ministry project related to the spiritual life. Given the transitions that he was facing and the lack of helpful resources, Jack decided to interview retired professionals to see if some common personal challenges in this phase of life might emerge. He regularly discussed the project with Jerry, who directs the Academy.

Jack's research intrigued Jerry, who had a background in pastoral counseling and years of experience as a pastor in Arizona. Jerry sensed the value of this work for the wave of baby boomers now entering retirement. He also had a personal interest as he plans to retire in a few years.

Our discoveries through the interview process excited both of us; we began asking what could be done with the information we had uncovered. Increasingly we felt that our findings were too valuable not to share. We consulted with others working in the retirement field, conducted workshops and seminars, and continued to talk to anyone who expressed interest in our learnings.

We had completed most of the research for this book before the fall of 2008, when the stock market took a nosedive and the United States officially entered a recession. We subsequently contacted all those we had interviewed to see how they were doing and to see if our content needed any adjustment. While some indicated added financial stressors, no one said anything that changed our conclusions about the personal dimensions of retirement in any major way.

Those of you who are not retired may feel that retirement is farther away than ever before due to current economic challenges. While this adds another challenge to retirement, it makes thinking and talking through the relational and vocational aspects of retirement all the more important.

Despite all we have learned, we confess a certain amount of anxiety about our own retirement. Each person's experience will be unique, filled with challenges and surprises. We hope, however, that this book will make retirement a bit easier for ourselves and for others.

INTRODUCTION

Retirement: The Personal Side

ADVICE TO THOSE approaching and already in retirement usually centers around finances, health and fitness, or desirable places to live. The underlying supposition is that retirement consists of endless recreation made possible by a big nest egg, good health, and desirable surroundings. This book looks at the more personal dimensions of the transition from working full-time to retirement, including relationships, feelings of self-worth and purpose, and spiritual and intellectual growth. These personal factors are central to our sense of well-being and fulfillment in retirement, just as they are in every other phase of adult life. We know this from our own experience and from studies of other stages of adulthood. In her book *New Passages: Mapping Your Life across Time*, Gail Sheehy identified changes in purpose, relationships, and spirituality as key issues to be worked through as we go through "middle life," which in her framework spans the age range of midforties through midsixties.[1]

Our insights about the personal dimensions of retirement grow out of interviews with forty-five retired professionals. Each had worked in a capacity that required a college education or equivalent (for example, teachers, doctors, nurses). In addition to the interviews, we tested and refined our findings through discussions with over one hundred other retirees in individual and group settings, as well as with those who serve this population in various capacities, such as pastors and financial advisers. We also brought our own experiences to bear. Jack is now in the early stages of retirement, and Jerry has served as senior pastor of a church with a large retiree population.

Taken as a whole, the conversations and interactions suggest an exciting and challenging picture of retirement. This time of life can be one of significant personal growth, as well as an opportunity to contribute further to one's professional field or to invest talents and experience in volunteer capacities. Clearly, moving from full-time work to retirement involves significant and sometimes painful adjustments in key relationships and in sources of self-worth. With some attention and effort, however, these aspects are usually worked through successfully in early retirement years.

We discuss the findings of our interviews, interactions, and experiences in terms of the personal transitions associated with moving from work life to retirement, including changes in sphere of influence, family relationships, and friendships (chapters 1–3). We also name opportunities for growth and service presented by this phase of life, including retiring to some area of service or contribution, spiritual and intellectual growth, and caregiving (chapters 4–6). And we discuss some of the primary personal challenges confronted in retirement, such as changes in personal identity, decline in physical capabilities, mortality, and preparing for the future (chapters 7–10). We then make some suggestions for individuals approaching and in the early stages of retirement (chapter 11) and for those who serve and enlist the services of the growing retiree population (chapter 12). The discussion questions at the end of each chapter may assist readers in thinking further about the topic introduced, or they could serve as a basis for group discussion. See also the annotated list of resources for both groups and individuals on the personal dimensions of retirement (Appendix A, page 103).

INTERVIEWS

We developed and refined an interview questionnaire in collaboration with current retirees and individuals who have studied other life transitions. Appendix B (page 109) includes the full questionnaire. Jack, who conducted the interviews, posed the same questions about the following topics to all participants:

1. the nature of their work before retirement and how they made the transition from full-time employment to part-time work or retirement.

2. how they invest their time and energy now that they are retired.

3. the impact retirement has had on their significant relationships, both inside and outside the family.

4. the effects of retirement on their feelings of self-worth.

5. the changes in spiritual interests and concerns they experienced as they moved into retirement.

Additionally, we asked participants to name organizations they are aware of that serve retiree populations and individuals contemplating retirement. Even though Jack asked interviewees the same questions, every conversation was unique in that it also included follow-up and clarification questions and interactions. This form of interview is called an "intensive interview."[2] It is characterized by a focus on each individual's interpretation of his or her experience at a deeper level than typical conversation between peers. We guaranteed participants confidentiality to encourage them to speak freely and honestly. Approximately one-fourth of the interviews have been in person and the remainder by telephone. While Jack knew a few of the participants prior to the study, most were recommended by other retirees, by pastors and priests, and by people serving retired populations. Each interview lasted from one to one-and-one-half hours and was recorded for subsequent analysis.

THE PEOPLE INTERVIEWED

The twenty-five men and twenty women we interviewed represent a broad range of executive and professional work experience. Nine were employed in the private sector; another nine were pastors or priests. Seven were professors or administrators in institutions of higher learning. Six were affiliated with not-for-profit or religious organizations, and six more were health care professionals (doctors, nurses, administrators). Three were state or local officials; three were authors; and two worked in primary or secondary education.

The interviewees also represented various ages at retirement, length of time retired, areas of the United States in which they had worked, family circumstances, and health. The average age of the participants upon retirement was sixty-two, which corresponds to the most recently reported average retirement age in the United States. The youngest at retirement was fifty and the oldest seventy. They have now been retired an average of six years, with the range being from six months to fourteen years. Their last positions before retirement were in twenty-one states, and some had lived abroad during part of their careers. About one-half had been married once, and the spouse is still living. A smaller percentage were divorced or widowed, and some of these had remarried. A still smaller percentage had never married. Well over half described themselves in good health, but others had experienced significant health problems either shortly before or since retirement.

Some characteristics were common to the participants. Most consider the spiritual dimension of life important. Most had a college education or equivalent. They seemed highly motivated and generally described themselves as self-starters. Undoubtedly some of these same characteristics were essential for their professions. As one participant said, "Retiring does not change who we are." Finally, while the individuals on average are probably somewhat more financially secure than the retiree population as a whole, these individuals represented a wide range of financial circumstances. In *The Graying of the Church*, Richard H. Gentzler Jr. noted that retirees of the baby boomer generation will be better educated and more well off than any previous generation.[3] Thus, our conclusions may offer a useful window into the future of retirement as well as into the experience of a significant subset of the current retiree population.

LIMITATIONS OF THE BOOK

First, this book does not comprehensively depict all stages of retirement. We focus on preretirement through what we call the middle retirement years. As a practical matter, preretirement and retirement together constitute several interrelated phases of adult life, which we find helpful to describe as follows:

1. *Preretirement,* the years leading up to retirement, in which one plans for transition from full-time work to no work or part-time employment.

2. *Early retirement years,* when physical capabilities may not differ markedly from the latter years of full-time employment, but changes in key relationships and sources of self-worth take place.

3. *Middle retirement years,* in which there is reduced mobility or other physical capability, but persons still find it possible to live independently.

4. *Late stage of retirement,* in which assistance from others is required for daily living, resulting in a change in living situation or amount of daily help in the residence.

The individuals interviewed were all in the second or third of these phases of preretirement/retirement. So while subsequent chapters may have some relevance to all of these stages, much of the discussion focuses on the first three of these stages.

Second, this book is not a comprehensive, quantitative social science study of retirement, from which quantitative conclusions can be drawn about retirement. Such a study could involve thousands of interviews and/or surveys with the broadest possible population of retirees. Instead, our work is qualitative, in that it identifies the most important personal transitions, opportunities, and challenges of this phase of life. To this end, we have employed generally accepted qualitative methods such as the intensive interview described above. The number of interviews carried out compares favorably with previous qualitative studies of other stages of adult development.[4]

Moreover, as noted earlier, the conclusions drawn herein are based on these interviews and as well as conversations with a much larger number of retirees and with individuals who serve this population. As a result, we feel confident of our conclusions' validity and believe that many of our conclusions apply not only to other professionals but also to a general audience of those entering retirement. Our conclusions deal with common human concerns such as relationships and self-image, not those related to work or profession.

QUESTIONS FOR REFLECTION

1. On a scale of one to ten, with one being the least important, how important to a fulfilling retirement are finances, health, and a desirable place to live? How would you rank relationships and sense of purpose as they relate to fulfillment in later life?

2. As you think back on earlier stages of your adult life, what challenges and areas of growth have you experienced during times of transition? In what ways is your experience consistent with Sheehy's description of the key issues of "middle life": purpose, relationships, and spirituality?

3. Which of the four stages of preretirement and retirement (page 15) are you in now? What additional characteristics of your current stage seem important?

TRANSITIONS

1

Finding Meaning in a Smaller World

RETIREMENT OFTEN SIGNIFIES a transition to a smaller world of authority or responsibility, influence, interactions, and recognition. In 1809, at age sixty-five, Thomas Jefferson made this transition from president of the United States to the overseer of Monticello, his beloved estate near Charlottesville, Virginia. Jefferson's biographies imply that he looked forward to this transition and made it with relative ease. In fact, one of the interviewees for this book, Brad, recalled that on a visit to Monticello he heard a tour guide say, "Jefferson got more satisfaction from this phase of his life, tending his garden at Monticello, than from his earlier responsibilities as the head of state." Jefferson also invested himself in numerous other pursuits between 1809 and his death in 1826, including spending time with his grandchildren, maintaining a lively correspondence with friends, and founding the college that has become the University of Virginia.

None of the people we interviewed has been president of the United States, but all moved to a smaller world upon retirement. Unlike Jefferson, many saw this "diminishment" as a key challenge of the first year or so after leaving full-time employment. For many of us, a successful transition to retirement means not simply learning to accept a smaller world but also finding our own Monticello garden to which we can devote ourselves in this phase of life.

A Smaller World of Authority or Responsibility

Tom, Phil, and Suzan were three of many retirees we interviewed who described leaving full-time work as a move to a smaller world of authority. Tom had held a variety of positions in which he supervised the work of other professionals. Such responsibilities had been an integral part of most of his adult life. In his younger years he had been a military officer and pilot, roles he found rewarding. But he also had a passion for urban planning and redevelopment. After leaving the military, he worked at progressively more responsible positions in cities around the country. In the years leading up to his retirement, he headed a large department in a major western city. From an office overlooking an inland waterway, he directed a team of attorneys, environmentalists, and planners. Tom's satisfaction with his preretirement life was both personal and professional. Almost a decade earlier, he and his wife were among the first professionals to move into the redeveloping downtown area; and now, in part because of his efforts and those of his associates, this downtown area had become one of the most sought after in the city.

While living in this vibrant area of downtown, Tom and his wife knew that they would retire to another part of the country, so they purchased a home in that place several years before he retired. And as the time approached, Tom looked forward to this life transition. After all, he reasoned, he would be free of the political pressures that are a part of almost any senior government role and could devote himself more fully to pursuits he had put off through the years.

Upon retirement Tom found to his surprise that he missed being depended on, directing others, having a tangible impact; he even missed the political environment. Sure, he and his wife had wonderful times taking trips together and visiting with grandchildren, but that only occupied a fraction of their time. He found that he was unable to find a worthwhile project or activity to which he could give himself. He even began questioning whether his decision to retire at the relatively early age of sixty had been wise.

Phil's professional life differed, but he expressed similar sentiments. Phil and a partner had started a manufacturing company in a small southeastern town more than twenty years ago, and the company had grown and prospered in the intervening years. His partner died unexpectedly after a few years, leaving Phil responsible for the company. He rose to the challenge. He enjoyed every aspect of building and running the company, from developing relationships with his employees to interacting with suppliers and customers in the United States and abroad. Still, Phil recognized the importance of passing ownership of the company to a younger person who could oversee its continued growth. An opportunity arose to do that and in a span of three days, he went from being company president and owner to just another resident of the town in which the company was located. He has no second thoughts about the decision. Nevertheless, he often feels sad when he thinks of leaving an endeavor in which he invested so much of himself. This feeling has heightened as time has passed and the company has done well with new leadership.

In our study, both men and women indicated difficulty in moving to a smaller world. Suzan worked intermittently as she raised her family and then reentered the workplace on a full-time basis as the head of a small private foundation. She loved this work and carried it out effectively. Her abilities attracted the attention of the leadership of the Protestant denomination to which she belonged and led to her recruitment as the first woman executive in the denomination. Four exciting and strenuous years followed, which she would not trade for anything. Still, as her term neared its end, she looked forward to setting her own schedule and being free of the almost continuous travel that her position required. She retired and within a few short months was bored with the lack of structure and stimulation in her life. In her words, she felt she had "flunked retirement." Less than a year after leaving her executive position, she took a new part-time position that used some of her skills.

A common thread runs through the experiences of Suzan, Phil, Tom, and others with whom we spoke. No responsibility or activity they engaged in during the early stages of their retirement drew upon their professional, leadership, or decision-making abilities and experience in any substantial or satisfying way.

A Smaller World of Influence

Other people described a second, somewhat different version of their smaller world of retirement, namely a more limited sphere of significant influence in the lives of other people. Every high school teacher and college professor we interviewed noted how they missed the interaction with students and the sense of positively influencing these young persons' lives. Rhonda taught in a public high school for thirty years. In a typical year she would relate to about one hundred sixty students. She recalled with pride her positive influence at critical times in the students' development and noted that she had left this big part of her life behind at retirement. The loss of this significant role motivated some of the retirees to assume part-time or other teaching responsibilities in retirement.

A Smaller World of Interactions

A third dimension of moving to a smaller world had to do with the loss of stimulating interactions with interesting people. Barbara articulated this loss with particular clarity. Prior to her retirement she oversaw fund-raising from individual donors and foundations for a major university. Her job involved close interactions with her subordinates, each of whom had fund-raising responsibilities in a particular geographic region. She thoroughly enjoyed her interactions with these people and the satisfaction of knowing that her leadership contributed to their success. She also had extensive one-on-one interactions with potential major donors and spent much of her time traveling around the country meeting and getting to know these interesting people. Still, she looked forward to retirement and to a more relaxed schedule. When it came, it devastated her in a way she had not foreseen. Most of the interactions that had become such a fulfilling part of her life ceased; in the early months of retirement, nothing took their place. In fact, during this period, her need for interaction led her to dine out alone in hopes of striking up a meaningful conversation with other diners.

Many others missed workplace interactions as well. Kathleen had responsibility for her company's educational programs. She retired early to care for an ailing family member and soon realized that she missed interactions with both the students served by this program and the instructors she worked with in preparing the courses. Carole served in a church leadership position in the years leading up to her retirement. She too was surprised by and unprepared for her feelings of separation from those she worked with and cared for. Moreover, to her surprise these feelings persisted for the better part of a year after she retired.

A SMALLER WORLD OF RECOGNITION

A fourth dimension of the smaller world is related to recognition and appreciation. Several of our interviewees had gone from positions of prominence in their communities to being simply another person on the street, in the neighborhood, or in the pew. The chief judge of a state circuit court, Jeremy often had his decisions and opinions reported in the local press. He spoke regularly at events in his community and around the state. Consequently, people in the community often recognized and greeted him. When he retired, not only did the press coverage, the recognition, and the invitations to speak come to an abrupt halt, but within a few months he found the activities he had looked forward to pursuing boring. In his words, "It did not take long for me to catch every fish I ever want to catch and fly every airplane I ever had an interest in being at the controls of." This combination of boredom and loss of recognition and appreciation caused him to begin asking "Who am I now?" and "What is my worth in this stage of my life?"

We discovered that religious professionals are not exempt from these feelings. Pastors and priests noted how much retirement had changed their sense of being known and appreciated. Tim, for example, observed that he felt constant affirmation of his importance and worth as the pastor of a church. He was shocked at how quickly his relationships and influence with former parishioners faded as they redirected their attention to his successor. Another pastor, Jake, had a similar experience. When people seem to look past him now, he feels like saying, "Hey, I am a pretty interesting person if you would take the time to get to know me."

This changing sense of being known and appreciated didn't apply to everyone. Edwin, a successful corporate executive who loved his work, was forced to retire when his company merged with a larger firm. His transition to retirement took place quickly and with little advance planning. However, he found it remarkably easy. Jan, who served in a clergy role prior to retirement, had a similar experience to that of Edwin. In her words, "It took me about five minutes to adjust to retirement."

Why do some people find moving to the smaller world of retirement so challenging, while others do it so effortlessly? The answer is not evident from either the interactions we have had or from previous studies of retirement or aging. At this point we can only point to several possible contributing factors. Those who moved from full-time to part-time work did not seem to experience the transition to a smaller world as acutely as those who stopped working altogether. Additionally, health played a key role for a few people. A smaller world was a welcome change for individuals with significant health challenges, affording them freedom and flexibility to accommodate their daily schedules and activities with regard to how they were feeling. Continuing activities they had enjoyed before retirement was a factor for both Edwin and Jan. Edwin continued teaching a course at a local university. Jan rekindled some of the artistic activities that had been important to her earlier in life but which she had put aside in recent years.

The larger question posed by the experiences we have described is this: How or where might I find fulfillment in this new smaller world of responsibility, influence, stimulating interactions with others, and recognition and appreciation? Or, using the experience of Thomas Jefferson, what will be my Monticello garden in retirement? Or, in the words of John, another of the pastors who was interviewed, "How do I acknowledge the real losses I face in transitioning to [the smaller world of] retirement while at the same time moving forward into this new phase of life alert and open to new opportunities and challenges?" Answering these questions requires time, thought, and effort. The good news from those interviewed is that most have made this transition successfully, meeting the challenge of moving to a smaller world by taking college courses, mastering new skills, and giving themselves in service to others.

Questions for Reflection

1. The authors identify four ways in which retirees feel they have moved successfully or unsuccessfully to a smaller world. These include (1) leaving a position in which others depend upon your judgment or expertise, (2) losing the sense of influencing positively the lives of other people, (3) severing interactions with interesting and stimulating people in the workplace, and (4) going from being a somebody to a nobody in the community. As you approach retirement, which of the above will prove most difficult for you? If you already have retired, which of these four or some other facet of moving to a smaller world best represents your own experience?

2. How would you respond to John's question: "How do I acknowledge the real losses I face in transitioning to [the smaller world of] retirement while at the same time moving forward into this new phase of life, alert and open to new opportunities and challenges?"

3. After the presidency, Thomas Jefferson significantly contributed to others' welfare and to his beloved Virginia. What legacy would you like to leave through the way you spend your retirement years?

CHAPTER

2

Navigating Family Relationships

Retirement can bring fundamental life changes, such as how much discretionary time we have and how we spend it, where our self-esteem comes from, and, as we saw in the previous chapter, the extent of our influence on and recognition by others. It is not surprising then that we also experience transitions in our most important relationships. This chapter will focus on how retirement affects key family relationships—with a spouse, siblings, adult children, and grandchildren. Then in the next chapter we will look at how retirement impacts friendships. We will see that these life changes can present both challenges and growth opportunities in important relationships.

HUSBANDS AND WIVES

Over half of the individuals we interviewed are married; the impact of retirement on relationships with their spouses varied widely. Tom is a retired business executive whose wife invested herself in community and volunteer activities after their children were grown. This couple described a modest change in their postretirement marriage relationship by saying that "it is an ongoing adjustment, a work in progress."

Frank gave a specific example of what this work in progress looks like for another couple. He retired from the life of a busy and successful physician two years ago, looking forward to the additional discretionary time afforded by this phase of life. He now realizes that he unconsciously expected that his wife would be available at a moment's notice for them to do the things and go to the places together that his schedule didn't allow for in earlier years. But his wife, who had retired a few years before him, already had developed a rhythm for her days and had made commitments to friends and organizations based on his long hours at the office. So, while they have a strong relationship and enjoy being together, they quickly discovered the importance of coordinating their schedules so that both have time for individual interests, as well as shared interests.

The importance of coordinating schedules as a part of adapting to retirement was mentioned as well by Jeanette, a retired minister. While she is fully retired, her husband still consults on a part-time basis. They schedule their individual activities on Monday through Thursday, so that they have a full three days available each week for travel and other activities they enjoy together.

Rhonda expressed another practical view of scheduling for retired spouses. She retired from her public-school teaching position four years after her husband's retirement from a university faculty position. In addition to planning for more extended times together, she and her husband have agreed on the meals they will share together. They routinely eat breakfast and lunch by themselves, usually at different times, and then share an evening meal together. They live by the maxim, "I married you for love, not for lunch," a distinct change from their working days when the time to share a meal had to be carefully guarded.

A more challenging version of the adjustment to the schedule and rhythm of retirement was described by Cliff, a retired pastor. Both Cliff and his wife had demanding professional roles prior to their retirement. They retired at the same time and moved to a new community. Cliff indicated that it took some time, communication, and patience to move from a life together built around work schedules to one with no externally imposed time commitments. Rod, a retired state government executive, took this one step further. He and his wife also retired at the same time. They found that their relationship in the early stages of retirement was sometimes strained not only by the absence of outside schedules but also by the reality that both were trying to figure out "who we are in this new stage of life."

Ruth described a good marriage becoming better after retirement. She spent the early part of her career as a classroom teacher, but over time moved to progressively more demanding leadership roles. By the time of her retirement she had responsibility for a large number of other professionals. Likewise, her husband had assumed progressively more challenging responsibilities over time. Both retired at the same time. For the first time since their early years of marriage they regularly had the time and energy to do things they enjoyed together, and they tended to get more pleasure out of these shared activities because of their reduced stress levels. Or, in Ruth's words, "It is almost like we got back the spouses we married, the ones who liked to have fun together."

Naomi, a retired physician, expressed a similar sentiment. She and her husband had a good marriage before retirement, and the additional flexibility in schedules allowed them to build on this foundation. Within the past year they took an extended trip to Europe, both for pleasure and to spend time with other family members. This shared experience of several weeks' duration would not have been possible while they both worked.

Roy, a retired business executive, described a more difficult adjustment in the marriage relationship after retirement. In their years of marriage, Roy and his wife had lived in several parts of the United States and abroad and had successfully navigated the stresses imposed on family life by the relocations. Both were looking forward to Roy's retirement. Nevertheless, they describe the years immediately after his retirement as "the most difficult of our married life." Why was this transition so hard for them? Roy feels that the primary contributing factors were a mismatch of expectations and selfishness on his part. His wife had expected him to be more available for them to do things together, while he was focused on objectives and activities he had looked forward to as part of his postretirement life. Unfortunately, they did not recognize this fundamental difference in perspective *before* the fact. They ultimately agreed to set aside two days a week as date days for doing things together and with friends. The good news is that over time their rocky relationship has been restored to health.

Paul, who had retired from a clergy role, described a different circumstance involving a rocky marriage relationship beyond retirement. His relationship with his spouse had been difficult in the years preceding retirement. Despite easing the flash points of money concerns and differing views on the value of pastoral ministry, retirement did not improve the relationship. In his words, "Our marriage was not made in heaven, and retirement did not change this reality."

A common theme that emerges from many of these accounts of adjustments to retirement or part-time work is the importance of communication about feelings and expectations. Another suggestion made by some is to arrange separate work spaces for husband and wife in the home, which allows each person to work independently on his or her own schedule.

SIBLINGS

In her book *Sisters and Brothers All These Years*, Lillian S. Hawthorne identifies retirement as one of the events of later adulthood with the potential to alter sibling relationships. Other events can change a relationship between siblings: loss of parents, declining health, as well as an inner revisiting and reevaluation of life and relationships. In the words of Hawthorne, "Longevity in itself does not guarantee sibling reconciliation or intimacy, but . . . [sets] the stage . . . to make it possible."[1]

Nearly a quarter of those we interviewed described this orientation toward closer relationships with siblings. Rick, a retired professor, noted more frequent phone and e-mail contact with his brother since retiring. Two other people noted that their relocation or that of a sibling so that they lived closer had created more time together. After retiring from pastoral ministry, Fran has had time to develop a closer relationship with a sister who lives in another community; they also share the bond of having become widows in the same year. Jennifer, a retired educator, travels several hundred miles every few weeks to visit a sister who is in poor health.

Interestingly, some individuals indicated that they had also grown closer to their siblings' children since retirement. Anna, a retired professor who never married, has always been close to her niece and family. This bond has increased since she retired. Tim, a retired pastor and one of nine siblings, has found himself becoming much closer to his brothers' and sisters' grown children in the years since he retired.

ADULT CHILDREN

The overwhelming majority of retirees with adult children reported improved relationships with them and with their children since retiring. The reason repeatedly cited was the additional time available to foster these relationships. Pat, a retired pastor, has an adult child whose family lives within easy driving distance. Consequently, Pat can give practical help, such as childcare when needed.

More typically, one or more children and their families live in a different part of the country than their parents. Maintaining these relationships requires extra effort: regular communication by phone and e-mail and periodic travel to spend time together. Roger described how this combination of visits and phone contacts has enriched his relationships with his daughters since he retired from his position as the senior pastor of a large church. This new closeness particularly pleases him because from his point of view and that of his daughters, his travel and work schedule earlier in life meant that he was not around for important events of their childhood and teen years.

David, a retired business executive, has sons with whom he has developed a stronger bond through regular phone contact and visits. Richard, a retired academic administrator, and his wife have sons and daughters in various parts of the country. They make it a priority to travel frequently to see each one and their families, as well as to plan time together every summer at their vacation home.

A few of the retirees interviewed have relocated to be nearer a son or daughter and their family. Nancy, a retired author, and her husband have a son in one state and a daughter in another. In a series of conversations the family together decided that Nancy and her husband would relocate to the area where her daughter and son-in-law live. Their daughter will be the primary caregiver as they age. George retired from his position as a university professor; he and his wife relocated to another state to be closer to their son and daughter and their families. Their experience of living nearby has been excellent. Judy, a retired physician, and her husband decided not to relocate to be closer to a son or daughter. Both their children have jobs that will necessitate periodic relocation, and they do not see themselves moving around to follow their kids. Jim, a retired city executive, and his wife had the unique experience of a daughter and her family relocating within a few miles of where they live. The ease with which they can now spend time together has made a positive difference in their relationship.

GRANDCHILDREN

"Grandchildren are the reward for not having killed your kids," one grandparent said while reflecting on the stormy teen years parenting his own children. Every individual with grandchildren articulated the priority he or she gives to these relationships. Or as one grandmother who is a retired denominational executive remarked, "My grandchildren are now my highest priority." The level of time, energy, and creativity devoted to the relationship with grandchildren is remarkable.

Jenny retired some years ago from her position as a college professor. At the time of her retirement, her grandchildren were still young, and during these years she cared for them often. Now they are in their teen years, and she is not as mobile as she once was. Nevertheless, she is a regular fixture at their athletic events, both home and away games. Making the effort to do this has allowed a continuing relationship with her grandchildren as they move through the teen years. Jenny particularly values this, because while working she often had to miss major events in her own children's lives. In her words, "I was not going to let that happen a second time."

Ray and his wife also have now been retired for several years. During most of this time their grandchildren have lived in another state. However, they have built strong relationships with the grandchildren by taking them on trips. This approach offers quality, one-on-one time while building memories that will last through the storms of adolescence.

Nancy and her husband, whom we mentioned earlier in this chapter, have adopted a variety of age-appropriate approaches to staying close to their grandchildren. They have granddaughters in their teen years who live in the same town as they do. They regularly have the girls and their boyfriends over for a meal or a cookout. With the younger children they plan a one-week summer camp at their house, tailored to the children's particular interests and ages.

OTHER FAMILY CONFIGURATIONS

Individuals and couples without children or grandchildren enter retirement with a somewhat different experience. They may feel left out as they hear their friends refer to "the kids." They may also wonder who will care for them when they need it. We suspect it is wise to consciously develop relationships with members of a younger generation. We mentioned Anna who had never married and had no children, yet in her retirement enjoyed her niece and her family.

Relating to children and grandchildren can be more complicated when they are stepchildren and step-grandchildren for one person. Spouses may feel varying levels of responsibility and connectedness to a particular child or grandchild because of differing history and relationship. In these situations, couples do well to spend time talking and negotiating issues, feelings, and loyalties, drawing upon the perspective of an unbiased third party if needed.

Family relationships, including spouses, siblings, children, and grandchildren, have a potentially enriching effect on our lives in retirement. The additional discretionary time we have in this phase of life allows us to invest in these relationships in ways that can deepen them. We encourage you to make this investment and find practical ways to grow in these relationships.

QUESTIONS FOR REFLECTION

1. Several interviewees indicated that retirement brought some adjustments in their relationship with a spouse. What are some particularly important areas for husband and wife to talk through before or in the early stages of retirement? What steps might be taken to bring differing expectations of the two into alignment?

2. Consider Lillian Hawthorne's observation (page 28) that some events of later life (retirement, death of parents, illness) can potentially draw siblings closer together. If you have siblings, how did your relationship with them change during the intense years of developing a career and raising a family? At your current stage of life how has your relationship with siblings changed?

3. Some retirees have relocated in retirement to be nearer children or grandchildren. What advantages or disadvantages would this approach have for you?

CHAPTER

3

Valuing Friendships

A COMMONLY ACCEPTED NOTION about growing older is that we become progressively more isolated and socially disengaged. And some of the scholarly work of the past few decades seems to support this conclusion. Recently, however, a different reality has come to light based on the largest and most comprehensive study of this topic ever undertaken. Benjamin Cornwell, Edward O. Laumann, and L. Philip Schumm's article "The Social Connectedness of Older Adults" shows that later life transitions such as retirement tend to prompt greater connectedness, particularly with "neighbors and through religious participation and volunteering."[1]

Our interviewees unanimously attach importance to strengthening existing friendships and building new ones for several reasons. Perhaps most important is the reality that our network of friends will change in retirement, whether we stay in the same community or relocate to a new one. Some friends will move to other locations by choice; others relocate because of ill health; still others predecease us. Most relationships forged in the workplace tend to fade after retirement and will need to be replaced. In all of these respects, friendship is a key area of transition in retirement.

This chapter will describe practical ways to navigate this transition, both by strengthening existing relationships and developing new friends. Some of the changes noted in friendships between men and women in this phase of life will also be explored. Then, we will consider some of the particular challenges associated with developing a new network of friends if relocating upon retirement.

Deepening Existing Friendships

When talking about friendship, almost all retirees we spoke with listed strengthening significant, long-standing relationships as their highest priority. This is most straightforward when these special friends live nearby. Norm, a retired corporate professional, and his wife decided to remain in the community where they had lived for over a decade before retirement. In the years when Norm and his peers were still working, they built relationships with one another by meeting weekly for prayer and Bible study. After retirement they expanded their weekly time together to include a golf game and lunch. In California, where they live, they can continue this meeting even in winter. These times move beyond Bible studies or golf games to sharing life's struggles and joys with one another. Norm considers himself fortunate to be so close to and invested in this group of friends. Several other men likewise identified participation in sports as a way that they maintain ties with friends in their area.

An even larger number of men and women identified church-related activities as a forum that deepens local friendships. Joan, a retired pastor, and her husband stayed in the same community when they retired. For several years prior to retirement Joan had met monthly with other pastors in the area, and they had become her close friends. As the time approached for Joan and one other pastor in the group to retire, the two considered whether to continue meeting with the group. They found that deep friendship trumps work status, so they have continued to meet and share their lives with one another. This group is a rich part of Joan's retirement experience. Similarly, as Christian education director at a church, Chris led a group of women in a weekly study, and over the years the members bonded. Since she also remained in her community after retirement, she has continued to meet with this group, some of whom are also now retired.

The importance of church-related friendships in retirement is by no means limited to former pastors or other church staff. Harry, a retired businessman, has remained in the same community in which he had worked. Since he retired, he has spent a significant portion of his time deepening his church friendships. This has taken many forms, ranging from traveling together, to meeting for coffee or lunch, to visiting every day with a peer who was dying of a rare form of cancer.

When our long-term friends live in other cities, states, or countries, the relationships require a different kind of attention (as do local friendships if we have mobility limitations). Sally, a retired executive of a nonprofit organization, provided a good example. She has a few close friends dating back to her college and early work years. These women have kept in touch with one another over a period of more than forty years through regular phone conversations, letters, and more recently e-mails and visits as often as possible. They have deepened their friendships while offering encouragement to one another in job and life transitions. Sally and her friends continue this practice in retirement with more ease, given the extra discretionary time.

James, an executive for a nonprofit organization before retirement, has developed and fostered an extensive network of friends through the years—both in his work setting and from church. Decreasing mobility has made it harder for him to meet others for a meal or to attend social functions. In the last couple of years, he has relied on creative support of these relationships through phone calls and e-mail. Others are making use of texting and social networking to sustain friendships (as well as family relationships with more computer-savvy relatives such as grandchildren).Technical changes that have had such an impact on the way we do business can also help us successfully sustain friendships as we age.

MAKING NEW FRIENDS

Most of the retired individuals we spoke with indicate that making new friends at this stage of life requires effort, taking initiative, and being alert to new possibilities for friendship. Or as one person said, "It is a lot harder [to make friends] now than when we had children at home and were interacting with other parents." Similarly, the retirees find they miss the ease with which they once met new friends through their workplace.

Those we interviewed suggested a variety of approaches to making new friends in retirement. Ruth, a retired nurse, described the importance of church as a source of new friends. She and her husband transitioned from city life to farm life when they retired, and in so doing became active in a different church. Their decision to "jump into this new church community with both feet" was critical to developing new friends to replace those they had left behind in their workplace and old neighborhood.

Still others noted the friendships that have developed as they have actively pursued their hobbies in retirement. Ralph, a retired business executive and an avid tennis player, has made several new friends by joining a tennis league after retiring. Before getting busy in her career, Donna painted a lot. She has used some of her time in retirement to rekindle this passion. She has gotten to know several other artists through the art school in which she has become active. Tom, a retired pastor with a lifelong interest in literature, regularly participates in a men's book club.

Community involvement has also provided new friends. Besides his tennis contacts, Ralph has gotten to know several people through community boards on which he serves. Judy, a retired rehabilitation specialist, has joined the local chapter of a club that fosters friendship among women in the community. She has become friends with several other women through the activities of this organization. One couple reflected on how they now reach out to people they do not know well. "We have given a lot of dinner parties since we retired," they said.

Still another source of new friends for several retirees is volunteer service or ministry in which they have become active. Tina is a retired nurse who became an instructor in the ESL (English as a Second Language) program offered through a church in her community. While she undertook this responsibility with the idea of serving others, it has also become a source of new friendships, including other instructors and some of the students. Will, a retired business executive, has had a similar experience in a hospital where he volunteers one day a week.

Finally, some women we interviewed noted a new sense of freedom in this phase of life to form significant friendships with men. Katrina pointed this out with particular clarity. She mentioned that when she was younger she felt that interactions with men had to be managed responsibly to avoid any inappropriate sexual attraction. As an older woman, she feels valued more for her personal characteristics than her appearance. She now counts a number of men of various ages as good friends. "A few wrinkles are a small price for the freedom of true friendship," she says. Observations of other retired women support those of Katrina. Several note that their circle of friends now includes more men than earlier in life. None of the men interviewed made a corresponding observation.

Challenges of Relocation to Social Networks

A 2007 article in the *Wall Street Journal* titled "Home and Family: Beyond the Nest Egg: What to Ask Yourself about Retirement; Key Questions Include: Go to Work or Not? Relocate or Stay Put?" was one of the first articles in the popular press to question the wisdom of relocating in retirement.[2] The authors noted that retirees often move to what they believe will be their dream location, only to find that it is more like a nightmare. The nightmare quality often hinges on their having left behind a network of friends without appreciating the difficulty of building a new one or a clear idea of how to go about it. In retirement, as in other phases of adult life, significant friendships are critical to a sense of connectedness and fulfillment.

About one-half of the people we interviewed have relocated in retirement. Of these, some moved to communities where they lived or worked earlier in life, while the others moved to communities where they have few or no friends. Individuals in both circumstances offered helpful and practical advice for such a move.

Most of the individuals who returned to a community in which they had previously lived found reconnecting with friends who still live in the area important and productive. The extent to which the reconnection is successful depends on the length of time they had been away and the turnover in the community to which they returned. Jane had been away from a community for a relatively few years before returning to retire. The network of friends left behind was still pretty much intact when she returned, and reestablishing these friendships was fairly straightforward. For those who had lived in the community at much earlier stages in their lives or professional careers, the picture differed. Tom and his wife had lived in a relatively transient community dominated by military personnel. After being away for about a decade, they returned to the area after retirement. They reconnected with a few former friends, but many had moved away. So their experience was more like moving to a new community than to one where they had previously lived. Jim and his wife had been away from the community to which they retired for over a decade, but the community has a more stable population. A large number of their friends still lived there, and they successfully reconnected with these people who had been important at an earlier stage of their life.

Tim provided another perspective on moving back to a community in retirement. After retiring from a career in state government, he and his wife moved to the town where he had grown up, but his wife had no real ties there. They found that his history in the community did not translate into a significant advantage for his wife's making new friends. Because they had no shared family ties, for her it resembled moving to a brand-new community.

A small number of those interviewed relocated to a community where other family members resided. Grace, an author and conference speaker, and her husband have enjoyed living in several parts of the country. However, she and her husband decided to retire in the town where a daughter and her family live, which has provided an easier transition than to a community where they know no one. Their daughter has introduced them to peers at church as well as elsewhere in the community. Grace and her husband have gotten a running start in making new friends as well as assistance in practical matters such as finding health care providers in the new community.

Jill retired to the town where her daughter, son-in-law, and granddaughters live. This arrangement has had a wonderful and unanticipated benefit. Some of the new friends she has made in this community are not peers in age but rather parents of other girls involved in activities with her granddaughters. These friendships have become a rich part of her social network.

It is hardest to build a new network of friends when we move to a community where we have not lived before and in which we have no preexisting ties. Don, a retired pastor who has held administrative positions in his denomination, has lived in numerous cities and towns around the country. Looking back over these moves, he and his wife concluded that making friends in a relatively newly built community is much easier than in a well-established one. In a newer community other people are also seeking friends. It is harder to break into a well-established community because people's "relationship plate is already pretty full." So Don and his wife elected to have "one more adventure" of moving to a new place; they selected a community that has experienced a large influx of new residents in the last four or five years. While it took effort to make new friends, they found this came about quite quickly. They felt at home in the new setting within six months of their move. Age and character of a community or neighborhood has an important bearing on the ease with which we establish new friendships in retirement.

Retiring to a community where we have not previously lived puts a particular premium on longtime friends who may live in other parts of the country or world. These relationships remain a priority to all of the interviewees. But for those who have moved to a new community, connecting with long-standing friends can be a lifeline. These connections give much needed encouragement and support as we make new friends. One person suggested that a line in an old Girl Scout song is particularly apt: "Make new friends but keep the old."

Of course, relocating in retirement affects family relationships as well as friendships. Among the individuals we interviewed who had relocated, some had moved closer to family members and others farther away. For the majority of these individuals, a feeling of "being at home" in a community seemed to have more to do with significant friendships than with proximity to family members.

Unique Challenge for Some Retiring Clergy

Some retired clergy sense the need to avoid interfering with their successor's leadership and ministry. This often means leaving the church they have served and sometimes involves moving to a new community. As a practical matter it also means leaving behind regular contact with former friends in the congregation. No one questioned the wisdom of getting out of the way of a successor. No parallel to this experience seems to exist in any other profession, however. No business executive, academic administrator, or educator sensed that he or she should relocate or leave friendships behind to make room for their successor. This raises the question for church and denominational leaders of how they can best accommodate the needs of incoming clergy to have minimal interference from predecessors while also being sensitive to the circumstances of their retiring clergy.

QUESTIONS FOR REFLECTION

1. How will you go about strengthening long-term friendships in retirement?

2. How can you get acquainted with new people on an ongoing basis in retirement, and how can you foster these new friendships?

3. How have your experiences affirmed Katrina's sense that friendships with individuals of the opposite sex are more straightforward for older adults?

4. What consideration have you given to the challenge of making new friends in the new place you will move to when you retire? Does taking on the challenge of building a new network of friends seem appealing or overwhelming?

OPPORTUNITIES

4

Retiring *to* as Well as *from* Something

THE BOOK, *Three Cups of Tea*, by Greg Mortenson and David Oliver Relin, is an inspiring account of the impact that one person can make on the world.[1] The book opens with a description of an attempt by a team of climbers to reach the summit of K2, the tallest mountain in the Karakoram range along the border between Pakistan and China. At 28,251 feet, K2 is second in height to Mount Everest but is considered by many to be the world's most challenging summit. Two members of the team reach the summit, but Greg Mortenson and one other team member forfeit their chance to do so in order to save another climber's life. Coming down the mountain after the rescue, Mortenson gets lost and ends up in the remote mountain village of Korphe. The residents of this village literally deliver him from death. But as he gets to know them in repeated visits, they give him even more—a purpose for his life beyond mountain climbing. He discovers that the village has no building in which to hold classes for its children. Instead, the children are taught in the open air, with the ground serving as a blackboard. Mortenson promises the village chief that he will build the children a school. The remainder of the book describes the remarkable odyssey of the fulfillment of his promise to this community and fifty-four others like it in remote regions of Pakistan and Afghanistan. What originally seemed like failure to Mortenson became the doorway to a life of extraordinary accomplishment for the sake of others.

In some important respects Greg Mortenson's personal journey parallels that of many retired professionals we have interacted with. They have spent most of their adult lives climbing the mountain of professional success. Whether they reached the professional peak they desired or not, in retirement these individuals have made remarkable contributions to the well-being of others. In fact, a number of these individuals view what they have done in this phase of life as their primary life accomplishment.

For some, finding a purpose in retirement results from prior planning and inquiry. But the larger number find meaning in retirement as a result of searching for ways to make their lives count in the years immediately after leaving full-time career pursuits.

CONTINUING CONTRIBUTION TO A PROFESSION

Several retirees who shared their lives with us continue to work part-time in their professional careers. Some have remained in consulting roles, using their expertise to contribute to the well-being of the company or organization. Roger is a retired scientist who spent much of his career with a medical equipment firm. He continues, on a part-time basis, to address challenging design and operational issues that require his extensive experience. Marge, a retired physician with particular expertise in federal and state regulations of disability benefits to injured and disabled individuals, has been retained as a part-time consultant to provide this expertise One of the coauthors of this book, Jack, has continued to work part-time for two of his former employers, assisting in research and development that may contribute to the future of space exploration.

All these retirees appreciate the opportunity to contribute to their professional field, to be stimulated intellectually, and to interact with their peers. The part-time nature of the work allows them to become more involved in volunteer activities or with their families. Added income is another tangible benefit.

Troy mentioned a different use of his professional knowledge after retirement. His expertise lies in developing tests of English as a Second Language (ESL), and his wife has an advanced degree in teaching ESL. Professionally, the two of them have been involved with ESL programs in the United States and abroad for many years. After full retirement for two years, one of Troy's former graduate students recruited them to start an ESL department at a new university in a Pacific Rim country. They spent two years working full-time there and had the satisfaction of seeing the new department become fully accredited. Even more fulfilling for them have been the relationships they formed with students, faculty, and administrators. Since their return to the United States, they have continued to advise university faculty and administration as well as to assist students from the university who elect to come to the United States for undergraduate or graduate studies. Troy and his wife describe this as the most rewarding experience of their lives.

In retirement Stan also is making a significant contribution related to his former career. He served as an executive in a large, multinational corporation. Among his responsibilities in the latter part of his career was the development of a leadership program for his company that focused on helping executives and professionals attract and mentor promising individuals from underrepresented groups. The program's success encouraged a local university to invite him to develop a similar program for the broader community at the time of Stan's impending retirement. He accepted the challenge, and today the program has grown into a statewide initiative that has graduated several hundred promising young leaders and opened new doors to underrepresented groups in a variety of professional capacities.

Not surprisingly, a number of former pastors and priests are now involved part-time in ministry with their denomination or organization. Richard was the first person to articulate a personal need to retire *to* something as well as *from* something. He came to this conclusion several years before retiring as he considered those things from which he derives satisfaction. These include in-depth interactions with other people, teaching, and exercising leadership—all important parts of his role as the senior minister of a large church. After retiring he took a part-time teaching job at a local university and accepted invitations to preach once a month. He also served on the board of a university in his early retirement years. These responsibilities have afforded him satisfying opportunities to teach, lead, and interact with people across a broad spectrum of ages.

Some of these working arrangements were in place at the time of the individual's retirement, as in the case of Roger and Marge. Others, like Richard and Stan, had basic arrangements in place when they retired that became fully developed over time. And, of course, the challenge Troy and his wife accepted had not yet appeared on the horizon when they retired.

CONTRIBUTIONS AS VOLUNTEERS

Many individuals described their contributions as volunteers. This work usually has no direct relationship to the field of expertise they developed while employed. Kent, for example, is a retired state official. About the time he retired, he and his wife attended a conference in an Asian country. There they met a local pastor who described the need for an orphanage in the area. After Kent returned home he began making plans to construct such a facility. He worked remotely, through the local pastor, to develop plans, oversee the construction of the initial phase of the facility, hire staff, and choose the children who initially would be served. He and his wife underwrote this initial phase with their own funds. Now the orphanage is fully operational, and Kent is raising funds from organizations and individuals to expand the facility to serve more children.

Randy is a retired corporate executive. In the months after retirement, he explored a number of volunteer possibilities and tried out a few of the most promising for a limited time. He finally decided to become a child advocate in the court system of his state. In this role he gets to know individual children and advocates for them as their cases proceed through the state court system. As evidence of his commitment to this program, he completed an extensive training program, followed by one year of working as a child advocate. Though Randy had no prior legal training, he finds fulfillment in this responsibility.

A number of individuals found purposeful activities tied to a serious medical condition they have faced. Barbara became an accomplished public speaker in her work leadership role, addressing large groups on an almost weekly basis. She also has a form of diabetes. After retiring, she was recruited by a national organization to travel and speak to patient and medical professional groups on the treatment and control of this condition, work she finds tremendously satisfying.

June is a retired oncology nurse. Two years after retiring she learned that she had a rare condition that required a stem cell transplant. After her recovery she began volunteering her time in the facility where she had been treated and is in the process of establishing a support group in her area for people with this condition. And Luke, a retired engineer, is also a transplant recipient. He works in the hospital where he received treatment and counsels transplant patients and their families. He is also on the board of an organization that serves this particular population.

Finally, the retirees we spoke with have undertaken a wide variety of volunteer responsibilities in church ministries. Their tasks range from substance-abuse counseling to pastoral care through programs such as Stephen Ministry to teaching and leadership responsibilities. Mark and his wife have lived in several parts of the world because of Mark's employment with a multinational corporation. Since retiring he has assumed the leadership of the overseas missionary program of his church, focusing on organizing trips by teams to carry out medical mission projects in foreign countries. He finds the work gratifying and feels that the responsibility allows him to exercise his leadership skills and prior overseas experiences. And his wife has become a part of an active women's ministry in an eastern European country, drawing upon the skills and knowledge she developed in raising a family in varied cultural settings.

Societal Implications of Retiring to Something

These examples of individuals who continue to contribute after retirement show the enormous potential of retired professionals. Not surprisingly, this potential is recognized by a variety of religious and other nonprofit organizations (as well as by some companies and government entities). To date, however, most organizations have not successfully recruited such individuals in significant numbers. When a connection is made between organizational objectives and individual interests or talents, it is most often the result of an individual's initiative or personal contacts.

These examples of older adults' unique contributions give credence to a proposal made in the early years of the Kennedy administration to establish a National Service Corps. This organization was envisioned as a domestic equivalent to the Peace Corps, with the purpose of mobilizing both young people and retirees to address urban and rural poverty. The president and the attorney general advocated the involvement of retirees in National Service Corps, both as a way to tap their reservoir of skills and also to add meaning to their lives through participating in service opportunities. In testimony before a Senate subcommittee, HEW secretary Celebrezze noted the large number of retired elementary and secondary school teachers, professors, health care professionals, attorneys, librarians, and social workers who could make a positive difference in the country through applying their expertise.[2] While the Peace Corps has been successful, the National Service Corps was never written into law, and the idea has not been seriously revisited in the intervening years.

Nevertheless, there is a strong connection between this proposal of almost fifty years ago and the desire expressed by retirees we spoke with. They overwhelmingly consider contributing to the well-being of others a priority, whether it be through a church ministry, community service program, academic program, or other service or creative activity. They perceive such activities as personally important as well, or in the words used in the 1960s, "adding life to our years." Michelle, a retired school executive, offered at least one reason for this orientation. "Look," she said, "I have been a self-starter all my life, and retirement does not change that." These retirees have contributed significantly to a field of endeavor in their working lives, and a satisfying retirement naturally involves a degree of continued contribution. This orientation toward continued service is a potential force for good in both individual organizations and in the broader society.

Questions for Reflection

1. How important is it for you to retire *to* something as well as *from* something?

2. What income considerations will you keep in mind as you reflect on part-time work after retirement, or will you give your time without payment?

3. What facet of your professional expertise would you like to use in service or ministry, or would you prefer to do something entirely different?

4. What area of service or ministry would you be willing to invest significant time and energy in? What stands in the way of this becoming a reality?

5. If you have no particular interest or passion for your retirement years but would like to explore a variety of potential opportunities, how might you go about this?

CHAPTER

5
_____

Growing Spiritually and Intellectually

EACH OF THE RETIREES we interviewed in-depth has worked in some professional capacity and actively participates in a church or other religious organization. For this reason we anticipated that some of these individuals would describe spiritual or intellectual pursuits as important in retirement. We found much more. The majority of these men and women indicate that they have experienced significant spiritual growth since retirement. A large number also describe a life of continuing intellectual development and remarkable intellectual contributions.

Several contributors to a volume on religious influences on the health and well-being of older adults noted the increasing frequency of prayer as we age and the ability of religion to help us face the challenges associated with aging.[1] Additionally, James A. Autry[2] and Harold G. Koenig[3] have written about the importance of spirituality in retirement in the broader terms of personal purpose, relationships, and the inner life. Continued intellectual development might be anticipated from the observation of Richard H. Gentzler and Craig K. Miller that the coming generation of retirees is the first to have grown up with the notion of lifelong learning.[4] And Marc Freedman has drawn a similar conclusion from the rapid growth of the travel-learning program Elderhostel over the past three decades.[5]

This chapter will describe why this phase of life is conducive to spiritual growth and some of the forms taken by spiritual growth in retirement. We will then look at examples of retirees' intellectual growth and contributions.

SPIRITUAL GROWTH

Our subjects most often cited flexibility and additional discretionary time in retirement as elements conducive to spiritual growth. Anna, a retired nurse, summarized the observation made by several people when she talked about the difference it made to her spiritual life to "not have to rush out the door to the job each morning and return exhausted each evening." Instead, she can set aside time daily for reflection, study, and prayer. As these practices have become a part of her daily routine, she has come to agree with Henri Nouwen's observation that "a life that is not reflected upon isn't worth living."[6] And for some others, the realities of declining health (theirs and others) and awareness of their mortality evidenced the importance of life's spiritual dimension.

The retirees spoke of several distinct forms of spiritual growth. As might be expected from Anna's comments, one form was the regular practice of spiritual disciplines such as meditation and prayer. Rebecca, who had done extensive speaking and writing on spiritual topics as a part of her profession, described how the time and freedom to practice spiritual disciplines regularly and in an unhurried manner has allowed her to "get to know God in a much fuller way." Jesse, a retired executive of a nonprofit organization, noted how greatly daily worship and prayer has enriched his spiritual life. Moreover, individuals indicated that the practice of these disciplines in a group, as well as alone, has been important. This was true for Trudy, a retired physician, who participated in the Academy for Spiritual Formation around the time of her retirement. Chris, who finds her spiritual life enriched by the freedom she now has to participate daily in the liturgy of her church, made a similar observation.

A second dimension of spirituality that blossomed after retirement was increased study of the Bible (or other sacred literature of one's faith). Ryan, a retired business executive, described how spiritually enriching it has been for him to participate in serious Bible study that involves both daily personal study and then weekly study with a group. Saul, a retired pastor, observed that his return to reading books on spiritual formation (an activity he had not pursued with regularity since completing a doctor of ministry program years earlier) has enhanced his spiritual growth. Andrew, a retired executive of municipal government, expressed the importance of his study of biblical archaeology to his understanding of the Bible's meaning. This emphasis on study as a part of spiritual growth caused some to link spiritual and intellectual growth.

Chris and others articulated a third manifestation of a growing spiritual life: the development of spiritually based relationships with a few other people. Since retiring she has had time to develop these relationships, which has played a role in deepening her spiritual life. Jamie, a retired college professor, said the same thing in different words as she reflected on the significance of deep kinship with people who make up for her a "church within a church." Ryan, a retired state worker, found relationships such as this in a covenant group in which he has been involved for over a year. Bill, who has only been retired for a year, stated that he now is looking for this kind of friendship.

Spiritual growth in retirement also manifests itself through the assumption of leadership and teaching responsibilities in a church or other spiritually oriented organization. In the previous chapter on retiring *to* something as well as *from* something, we noted how Mark has felt called to assume responsibility for the missionary program of the church that he and his wife attend. Ryan has assumed a part-time position at his church, overseeing the pastoral care of the congregation.

A number of those we interviewed suggested that this period of spiritual growth has resulted in a refinement of their personal theology. This seemed particularly true of individuals who had retired from pastoral or denominational leadership responsibilities. Johanna is one such person. When she worked full-time, she tended to avoid confronting the hard questions and relied instead on partial understanding from the past. Studying the Bible more systematically in retirement has given her the opportunity to seek greater understanding. Others mentioned that their theological perspective has broadened and become less sectarian as they have been freed from daily pastoral or administrative responsibilities.

Intellectual Growth and Contribution

Among the retirees we interviewed were men and women pursuing intellectual growth through formal courses, personal study, and participation in educationally oriented travel. Tom, a retired denominational leader, is improving his foreign language skills through an online course, and he has completed a similar science course. Some are among the growing number of retirees participating in lifelong learning programs at local universities, as is one of the authors (Jack). Together, three universities within sixty miles of where he lives serve well over a thousand retired students. Jean described a trip to eastern Europe that she had recently taken. She selected this tour not only because she had always wanted to visit the region but also because the leader was an acknowledged authority on the region. She described the intellectually stimulating lectures he gave as the tour group visited sites of historical and cultural significance.

Several people related taking on significant teaching responsibilities in retirement. Over 10 percent of the people we interviewed have taught or are teaching part-time at the college level in retirement. Some were faculty members prior to retirement, while others have developed areas of expertise that are now in demand. Wayne, a retired business executive, began teaching a course on investing at a local university while still working and has continued to do so in retirement. In addition, since retirement he has developed a course on electronic commerce, which he now offers at the same university.

While the learning and teaching activities are impressive, the creative activities that these retirees have undertaken are equally so. Several people we talked with are engaged in writing projects. Mike, one noteworthy example, feels that a part of his calling in retirement is to write two books that his life of scholarship has prepared him to offer. One is now finished, and the second in process. Reviewers of the first book have told Mike that this may be the best work of his life. So much for the view that retirement is an unproductive period!

George, another retired professional, is making substantive intellectual contributions. He has used his knowledge of mathematics to develop a fundamentally new stock-trading methodology. This body of work has been lucrative for him; he lectures on it at universities, and it is the subject of a forthcoming book.

Ann did not pursue a career outside the home during the years her children were growing up. Later on, however, she began speaking and writing. Now that she is retired, she has become a prolific writer, having recently had two books published and is currently working on a third.

Still others have undertaken substantial creative activities for their own benefit and that of their families. Several individuals are recording family histories for their children and grandchildren.

These activities and contributions suggest that retirement can be an intellectually active and productive time in which we learn as well as teach others. Our interviewees enthusiastically affirm that creative activities are a source of enjoyment and fulfillment in retirement.

Earlier we noted that Thomas Jefferson apparently enjoyed the years following his retirement from the presidency. Some have suggested that he considered his most valuable contribution in this period of his life to be the founding of a college that is today known as the University of Virginia. You and I may not accomplish anything so notable in retirement. Nevertheless, an orientation toward continued spiritual and intellectual growth can make this portion of our lives as fruitful as any other. This mind-set, along with the maturity and experience we now have, can result in actions and relationships in retirement that can become the most valued of our entire life.

QUESTIONS FOR REFLECTION

1. How much time, energy, and effort did you expend preparing for your profession? What investment of time and energy are you willing to make to prepare spiritually and intellectually for retirement or to enrich this phase of life if already retired?

2. What dimensions of spirituality mentioned above—meditation and prayer, Bible study, spiritual friendships, leadership, and service—especially draw you? What steps might you take to foster these areas of your spiritual life?

3. What opportunities for continued intellectual growth and contribution appeal to you? How can you turn these opportunities into reality?

CHAPTER
6

Responding to the Call of Caregiving

We often heard from interviewees that the reality of retirement differs from the myths perpetuated by our culture. This time of life offers more than the carefree existence portrayed in advertisements for products ranging from travel services to investment products, in which we do our own thing on our own schedule according to our own plan. The dichotomy between myth and reality is nowhere more evident than in the lives of individual retirees who have responsibility for the care of a loved one. Approximately one-third of the retirees we interacted with have had significant caregiving responsibilities since they retired. And, contrary to the popular view that such responsibilities when they arise are the purview of women only, both men and women described experiences of giving care to a loved one.

This chapter considers a number of circumstances in which care for a loved one has been a significant part of retirement. We will highlight some of the challenges this responsibility presents. We will also indicate how individuals with such responsibilities view them as an opportunity or a calling rather than a detour.

CARE FOR A PARENT

Caring for a parent or parent-in-law is the most frequent type of caregiving mentioned by both men and women. The retirees usually anticipated taking on this responsibility. Rhonda was a college professor prior to her retirement. In the years since she left the university she has been the primary caregiver to both her mother and, at different periods, to her mother-in-law and father-in-law. Likewise,

George, who retired from a leadership position in a nonprofit organization, has had caregiving responsibility for both his own mother and his spouse's mother. Rhonda's husband is deceased, and George's wife still works full-time, so in neither case could a spouse share these responsibilities. Rhonda did receive assistance from siblings in caring for her mother-in-law and father-in-law.

Three other retirees, Pam, Rich, and Mary, cared for one parent. Pam is a retired nurse, and after her retirement she served as her mother's primary caregiver for a significant period of time. Rich retired from a position as senior pastor of a church. Since that time his mother's health has deteriorated to the point that she now resides in an assisted living facility. He provided care while she remained at home, helped her with the transition to the new facility, and continues to visit her often. He takes care of her business affairs and helps out in other practical ways. Mary has cared for her mother as her dementia has grown progressively worse, helping her move from an assisted living facility to a nursing home. Mary finds that her mother's current condition causes her to wonder *Is this what is in store for me as I approach the end of life?*

CARE FOR A SPOUSE

Several individuals described caring for a spouse. Kathleen retired from her position as an educational program coordinator to care for her husband. Nate, who has been retired from the pastorate for several years, provides care for his wife as her activities become more limited by a form of dementia. Wayne is a retired business executive whose wife now suffers from a neurological disorder that progressively limits her physical activities.

All three of these individuals and their spouses live a more challenging and lonelier retirement than they had envisioned. Kathleen had planned to participate in the lifelong learning program of a local university in her retirement, but the demands of caregiving have caused her to postpone this and other activities. Nate spends more time caring for his wife and less time building and sustaining friendships than earlier in retirement. Wayne's friendships also are suffering. He finds this a lonely time for him and his wife, with fewer people coming by to visit and fewer invitations from others to engage in activities outside their home compared to the years when she was well. He understands this, because their friends know that they cannot predict in advance how his wife will be feeling. But the experience is hard nevertheless. For the same reason, they can no longer plan extended travel. Perhaps most difficult is that they can no longer work together in an area of ministry and service they had enjoyed earlier in retirement.

RESPONSIBILITY FOR AN ADULT CHILD

Upon retirement from her academic position, Jean relocated to a smaller community some distance away to help her adult daughter develop a new business. Shortly thereafter, her daughter had an automobile accident and sustained serious injury that required a prolonged period of recovery and has resulted in some permanent disability. Immediately after the incident Jean cared for her daughter on a daily basis. Her daughter has now recovered to the point that she no longer needs continuous care, but Jean still helps her with her business and other matters.

Jean could not have anticipated the accident and its consequences, but its impact on her, as well as on her daughter, has been significant. Her move to the new community was a big transition, requiring Jean to build a new network of relationships while caring for her daughter. She wisely decided to continue fostering her network of relationships prior to retirement. These friends from the past have given tremendous support to her in this combined transition and caregiving period. Her ongoing involvement in areas of ministry with her church has also sustained her during this time.

Many other men and women told us about caregiving responsibilities they have for an adult son or daughter. Two couples cited circumstances in which mental illness prevents a son or daughter from being a fully functioning adult. Ian and Beth's daughter lives on her own but cannot fully manage her own affairs or hold a job that supports her. They have helped her buy a house within a few blocks of them and provide financial support and assist her with a range of other business and personal matters. As in Jean's case, this responsibility has been a part of what they view as fulfilling and productive in retirement.

SURROGATE PARENTS FOR GRANDCHILDREN

While grandchildren are a source of joy for many retirees, some have had to assume greater accountability for these children. Rick, a retired physician, is one example. Within a year of the time he and his wife retired, their daughter and son-in-law could no longer care for their two small children. No other family member could take in the children, so Rick and his wife have become the children's surrogate parents. The experience has been demanding physically, has placed financial demands on them that they had not planned for, and has constrained the freedom they expected to have at this age. While they currently can fulfill this obligation, they realize that as they age physical limitations may reduce their ability to parent these children. For this reason, they continue to seek other family members who may be able to help care for the children as they move into their teen years.

Other retirees we have spoken with provide day care for their young grandchildren. Judy, a retired nurse, lives in the same city as her daughter and son-in-law. For three years after her retirement, she cared for her grandchildren every weekday, which permitted her daughter and son-in-law to work full-time. She continued to provide this care until illness required hospitalization and a prolonged recovery.

Caring for grandchildren is a blessing for both grandparents and grandchildren; it allows them to get to know each other better. However, the grandparents in these circumstances realize that their age and energy level limit their ability to serve as surrogate parents.

CAREGIVING AS A CALLING

The circumstances of the caregivers described above vary widely. The duration of their responsibilities ranged from a few months to years and has involved everything from day-to-day responsibility to intermittent assistance when needed. We normally expect to care for a parent, but caring for a spouse, an adult son or daughter, or a grandchild can come as a surprise. Every case has involved hard times and real sacrifices. Still, across this wide variety of circumstances, the retirees giving care have uniformly looked at this responsibility more as a calling than as an unwanted interruption. This frame of mind has allowed them to maintain a positive outlook and to give care graciously. Their outlook has benefited them and their care recipients.

What has allowed these retirees to approach difficult responsibility with such grace? While no single answer suffices, their descriptions of these experiences suggest several factors. One has been love for the person cared for. As one individual with responsibility for a spouse said, "It is impossible to imagine doing this for someone you do not love." Some have also mentioned the role of personal faith in helping them see this service to a loved one as God's best for them at this time. Many of these caregivers have also worked to sustain key friendships and important activities, albeit on a more limited basis. Finally, as stated most explicitly by those caring for grandchildren, the caregivers have been honest with themselves about what is and is not realistic.

QUESTIONS FOR REFLECTION

1. When have you experienced significant caregiving obligation for a loved one? What was it like for you? What did others do that you found helpful in carrying out this responsibility?

2. As you look ahead, what family circumstances suggest the possibility of your becoming a caregiver in the future? How might you prepare for this responsibility? What steps do you envision taking to ensure your emotional and physical health?

3. Whom have you known who honestly sees caregiving responsibilities as a calling rather than a detour? What lies at the heart of this positive outlook?

4. At some point you may require care. What attitudes might allow you to receive care with grace and thanksgiving?

CHALLENGES

7

Who Am I Now That I'm Retired?

WE HAVE DESCRIBED a broad range of changes associated with retiring from a life of work. These changes include how we spend the majority of our time and effort, the amount of discretion we have in our schedule, the responsibilities we may assume, and the dynamics of key family relationships and friendships. Subsequent chapters will highlight other changes as retirement progresses, including increased physical limitations and the need to plan for some level of assistance in living and the realization that our lives are of limited duration.

Because of the range and extent of these changes, a key challenge for many of us in living a fulfilling retirement life is developing new sources of significance and feelings of self-worth. We explored with each interviewee what gave him or her a feeling of significance before retirement and what now gives that feeling in retirement. Most retired professionals described vocation, position, and career as being somewhat important in how they think of themselves, though the centrality of these elements to feelings of significance and self-worth differs from one person to another. The real question is to what extent do these changes in status and sources of self-worth represent a change in identity?

RETIREMENT AND PERSONAL IDENTITY

Work defines us in many ways; it expresses our values, goals, gifts, and relationships. To say in a social setting something like "I'm an engineer" or "I'm an attorney" or "I'm a priest" offers a shorthand description of ourselves to others. Our vocational identity opens the door for further conversation ("What kind of engineer?" or "Who did you work for?"); or it closes the door, and we move on to other topics. Often, when we ask a person we are meeting for the first time, "Who are you?," we are really asking, "What do you do for a living?"

The retirees we interviewed saw this loss of a ready-made self-introduction as reflective of a deeper question: Who am I now that I'm retired? For some, the loss of position or title was significant. Surprisingly enough, we did not find a major difference between how the women and the men we interviewed looked at the loss of professional identity, possibly because the majority had professional roles that demanded much of them and from which they derived satisfaction. At the same time they consciously sought to balance attention to profession with other areas of life (family, friends, other interests) prior to retirement.

We also found that, over time, most of these retirees have developed new ways of thinking about themselves (as well as introducing themselves) that transcend their former vocational identity and are more oriented to the present and future. A conversation with Sheila quickly focused on how she helps less able residents where she lives. Ted passionately embraces his writing. Mark expresses excitement about his next medical mission trip to India. Jack, one of the authors of this book, who is partly retired, feels good about working with other retirees to identify ways to make this phase of life fulfilling and productive.

CONTINUITY/DISCONTINUITY

Does retirement present an identity crisis? *Crisis* seems too strong a word for what we heard from those we interviewed. Clearly, a transition takes place, an internal and external shift of varying magnitude. For most, however, retirement did not present the pronounced crisis that midlife sometimes brings. These folks already have experienced various crises and dislocations and have shaped themselves around adjustments such as the kids' leaving home or the arrival of the first grandchild. While some experienced an acute sense of loss at retirement, they did not appear to experience the kind of hidden turmoil of the adolescent or midlife variety. Generally, retired people don't add the fuel of their own suppressed or repressed personal agenda to the fire of this transition. Some grieved their vocational years more than others—the loss of collegial relationships, the engagement and challenge of work, a regular paycheck—but none of those we interviewed seemed motivated to redefine themselves with red sports cars and trophy spouses. A different and inherently more productive identity shift seemed to be going on.

Retired professor Tom said it well, "Retirement is not a new beginning. It's more like pulling together the values and dreams and projects that have not been done and finding a way to do them now." Often those we interviewed seemed to search for a sense of continuity with the past rather than attempting to dislocate themselves from it. Integration may be more important than innovation. The urge seems to be, "Now, with the time I have, I want to invest myself in ways that reflect what I value and believe in." This approach is consistent with previously reported observations of Gail Sheehy and others, who point to the later phases of life as integrative in nature.

So the search that takes place in life beyond a consuming, full-time career is not to find a new self but to become who we really are in a fuller and more complete way. Joan Chittister expresses this sense of continuity when she writes, "It is a very comforting feeling to know that age does not change us. On the contrary. In some ways, we are all just getting to be more of who and what we have always been."[1] Or as one interviewee put it, "You're really the same person inside."

IDENTITY CHALLENGES

While we found continuity of identity in those we interviewed, we also discovered the dynamics of adjustment. Retirement may not trigger an identity crisis, but it raises major questions and invites new responses.

Feeling Lost

While a sense of relief and freedom from hectic work schedules and organizational demands accompanies the early months of retirement, several of our respondents commented on feeling a bit lost, wondering what to do with their free time. "What next?" we heard, either out loud or between the lines. Organizations define individual agendas; without them, we may not know how to proceed, at least for a time.

This time of drifting without a clear purpose pushed many to seek a more spiritual identity. We have talked about the hunger many retirees have for spiritual and intellectual growth. The identity issue may be expressed with some questions: Am I a human *being* or a human *doing*? Do I define myself primarily by what I *do* or by who I *am*? Who tells me who I am?

This desertlike encounter with emptiness and loss can be valued as a positive experience or at least a fruitful and necessary one. Several retirees with whom we talked rushed into heavy volunteer schedules that left them feeling dissatisfied. "It's easy to be busy," Joe said, "and hard to feel engaged." Other retirees seemed to distract themselves with travel and entertainment, and still others quickly returned to work on a part-time or even full-time basis. The retirees in some of these circumstances miss the opportunity to grieve the old work-related identity and prepare for new endeavors.

While feeling a bit lost was common for the retirees we talked to, usually this experience was followed by some newfound sense of purpose. We know some who lingered in a time of discernment, asking themselves where and how they wanted to be engaged. Others were given a purpose that defined them, not of their own choosing but which they accepted willingly. John, for example, was unsure what to do with himself in retirement. When a family member needed a caregiver, he found his place of usefulness. His identity radically differed from what it had been while he worked, but to him this new role of caregiver was more compelling.

Accepting the Past

One way we identify ourselves is by telling the story of our life. What happens when that story includes difficult chapters, clear failures, or deep regrets? How do we tell our story then? How do we free ourselves to engage in the present and maintain hope for the future?

Richard Morgan and others believe that telling our story as we age is an essential life task. In doing so, we look for meaning in the context of the history we have lived through and the larger spiritual dimensions. In his book *Remembering Your Story: Creating Your Own Spiritual Autobiography*, Morgan suggests we begin with a simple life review, jotting down memories of each decade we've lived. Creating a "life graph" or time line offers some sense of order and movement to our life journey. From this baseline, we can explore particular seasons and relationships as they have unfolded. We can then revisit painful memories and disappointments with the knowledge that the bigger picture of our life is more than these places of pain.[2]

Several of those we interviewed acknowledged the challenge of coming to terms with the past and finding a sense of resolution or peace. Trent, a retired minister, is alone among his siblings in not having earned a Ph.D. degree. In the years when he could have pursued this option, he chose instead to spend the time with his family and ministry. But in retirement he spends more time interacting with these siblings, which forces him to face his perceived failure on a regular basis.

Others questioned why they chose the vocations they did. Still others expressed regret about opportunities missed. Some simply wanted to remember their lives and savor the blessings. Seeing life as a whole, in the larger perspective of past, present, and future, is an important part of coming to terms with identity in retirement. Rather than focus on the work we once did, in retirement we now try to give the world our dreams, our hopes, our legacy—that becomes our identity now.

When we began interviewing retirees for this book, their openness surprised us. Retired people welcome the opportunity to tell their story, review their life journey, and ponder questions of relationship and significance. Our sense is that many retirees long to be identified as something more than "retired," because their identities are so much more interesting and diverse. To the extent that our culture tends to discount older adults, we miss the opportunity to recognize them for the unique individuals they are.

QUESTIONS FOR REFLECTION

1. What aspects of your life give you a feeling of significance? How, if at all, have you sensed these aspects changing in recent years?

2. How do you usually introduce yourself to others? What do you want people to know about you from a first interaction?

3. The authors highlight identity shift as a time that can be both desertlike and can inform insightful personal growth. As you think back over transitions you have experienced, in which have you experienced both feelings of being lost and then, in retrospect, a sense of real personal growth?

4. What memories energize you for the present and for the future? Which ones give you a sense of identity? Consider recording serious regrets to gain a sense of perspective or talking about them with a trusted friend or a professional. Consider this thought from Joan Chittister, "When we rethink our past choices, the central question is if everything in us that needed to develop as a result of each choice, did."[3] What growth have your past choices fostered?

CHAPTER

8

Meeting Declines in Physical Capabilities

MESSAGES LIKE "SIXTY-FIVE is the new fifty!" turn up everywhere these days, from books on life transitions to advertisements for brokerage firms. There is some truth to such a characterization of growing older in our time. Over the past few decades, medical care and, to a lesser extent, nutrition and exercise have substantially increased average life expectancy. The typical level of physical activity in retirement appears to have increased as well. While the individuals interviewed for this book are the beneficiaries of these trends, they also realize that their physical capabilities will decline as their retirement progresses. In this chapter we will see how this awareness motivates them to plan for the future in practical ways. We'll also hear their concerns about how to accept increasing physical limitations with grace and optimism.

The retirees we spoke with noted three facets of this eventual physical decline. Those who have been retired for a relatively short time and are still in good health emphasize the need to focus their reduced energy levels on the important matters. Both younger and older retirees commend doing early in retirement those things that require a high degree of mobility. And those who are older or have physical conditions that limit their activities articulate the challenge of maintaining a positive outlook.

REDUCED ENERGY LEVELS

James had been a successful corporate executive. Before retirement he led a variety of civic activities as part of his company's commitment to improving its community. He did this so well that he was asked to continue in this role after he retired, and he obliged. Within three years, however, he became conscious of some decline in his energy level. In his words, "In most of my professional life I was able to burn the candle at both ends for days on end without a noticeable adverse effect. It is simply not that way any longer." As a result he dropped some of his community responsibilities in order to give his full attention and energy to those he considers most important. Although James's decline in physical capability was small, he noticed it; and it motivated him to focus his abilities on those areas that he felt were a priority.

THE CHALLENGE OF DIFFICULT OR STRENUOUS ACTIVITIES

Like James, Dorothy also was a prominent leader in a large organization prior to retirement. She has now been retired about four years. In that time she has come to realize that she has perhaps an additional decade of relative independence and good health followed by a period of lesser physical capability and increased dependence on others. While acknowledging that no one knows how long he or she will be able to undertake particular activities, Dorothy has decided to concentrate in these early years of retirement on those activities that are only possible with her present health and energy level: entertaining large groups of friends and family and strenuous travel. Just as James's decrease in stamina caused him to be more selective in how he invests himself, Dorothy's sense that her physical condition will not always be as it is today has helped her focus on certain types of activities now.

A number of individuals expressed interest in the concept of doing now what you might not be able to do later. Jan owned a travel agency prior to retirement. While still working, she had advised others on the importance of undertaking physically demanding travel while still healthy. She has now been retired for a number of years. She can no longer do the kind of traveling she enjoyed when first retired and so is experiencing personally the wisdom of her advice to others in her former profession.

Accepting Reduced Capabilities

Several people spoke of the challenge of accepting decreased capability they already had experienced or, because of family medical history, expect to experience as they continue to age. Some also reflected on how they are meeting this challenge.

Peter, a retired minister, spoke about the challenge of decreasing capability, which has been brought into clear focus by two realities. The first is his progressively worsening arthritis. The second is his concern about the future: many older adults in his biological family experience a form of dementia, and likely he will as well. He is realistic about the losses he already has experienced and those yet to come, but he is equally clear about the need to "age gracefully by accepting each day and its challenges as a gift." Reflection on his life as a pastor has brought the realization that he is most influential and helpful to others when conversing with them one-on-one. Despite his decreasing mobility, he still has opportunities for these interactions. He also uses the phone and e-mail proactively to sustain important relationships even when he can no longer visit in person.

Other individuals highlighted ways they work around their limitations. Ted, a retired executive director of a nonprofit organization, also has mobility limitations. Like Peter, he relies more on e-mail and the telephone than personal visits to stay connected with a large circle of friends and former colleagues. Jean, a retired teacher, also has limited mobility. But she describes her situation now as "rich with friends." Many of her current friendships have come through her church, which does an excellent job of helping her stay as involved as she can, and through her involvement in her grandchildren's activities and the opportunities there to get to know other parents and grandparents.

Beyond the Life Stages of Those Interviewed

The individuals we interviewed were in their early and middle retirement years. So while some had experienced reduced energy levels and mobility, few had faced the hard decisions that often come in later retirement years. These may include moving from a private residence to an assisted or long-term care facility and surrendering driving privileges.

QUESTIONS FOR REFLECTION

1. The authors note that improved medical care, nutrition, and exercise may increase life expectancy and physical capabilities at any age. What lifestyle changes have you made in retirement to live the most active life possible?

2. What accommodations, if any, are you making for experienced changes in your physical capabilities?

3. What in your family history makes you anxious about your physical capabilities as you age?

4. Who within your family or circle of friends is meeting his or her declining physical capabilities with grace and optimism? To what do you attribute this positive attitude?

CHAPTER

9

We Won't Live Forever!

THE PEOPLE OF ANCIENT Egypt seem to have been preoccupied with death and preparation for the life thereafter. Visiting the pyramids of Giza or the temples and the Valley of the Kings near Luxor or even viewing artifacts from King Tut's tomb reveals the attention rulers of this ancient society gave to death.

We are not as attentive to the afterlife in our modern society. Although Benjamin Franklin is quoted as saying, "In this world nothing can be said to be certain, except death and taxes," we live much of our adult lives as if we are not so sure about the death part. It seems like a distant reality except, perhaps, when a grandparent, parent, or other older relative dies. Several of the men and women we interviewed for this book, however, pointed out that they have become more aware of their own mortality in their retirement years.

GROWING REALIZATION OF MORTALITY

The most often cited reason for a growing awareness of mortality is the death of friends or loved ones. The majority of those interviewed had lost one or both parents, and others had experienced the death of a spouse, sibling, or friend who was a contemporary in age. Such events, relatively rare earlier in life, occur with increasing frequency as we age.

Another major reason for awareness of one's own mortality was illness. Some of the individuals we spoke with had their first personal experience of serious or potentially life-threatening illness since their retirement. Facing the real possibility of the end of one's own life and having time for reflection during recovery from such a condition contributed to an increased awareness of mortality. For others, it was not so much a single event of serious illness but the increasingly frequent occurrence of less serious health problems after retirement that brought a raised awareness of mortality.

Though not mentioned as often as death of others or illness, some individuals were reminded of their own mortality by encounters with circumstances that they could not control: illness of a loved one, divorce of an adult child, or another difficult situation.

Living Each Day as a Gift

One by-product of awareness of our mortality is an appreciation for the importance of each day. For Ted, a retired pastor and academician, the later years of his professional life were busy. He retained his preretirement pace in the months following his retirement. Then, during Ted's annual physical, his doctor discovered a serious medical problem that required major surgery, an extended period of recovery, and attendant limited activity. Even though Ted eventually returned to good health, this experience profoundly affected his outlook. In his words, "I used to take every new day for granted. Now I realize that each new day is a gift of God's grace; and it is this day I need to focus on. It is full of possibilities—not just responsibilities—for relationships and for surprises." Moreover, Ted's realization that he belongs to God in life and in death permits him to anticipate death and to consider how to help his younger loved ones see his life and death in this way as well.

This significant transition in Ted's personal perspective has transformed everyday events in his life from obligation to opportunity, brought personal fulfillment, and the ability to be fully present in the moment for others.

Others expressed a growing awareness of the importance of each new day, though it was not always as explicitly tied to feelings of mortality. Jean also held a demanding leadership role in church ministry. In her words, "One of the great personal benefits of coming off the fast track is learning to be fully present in today." She is discovering that this change in orientation contributes in a major way to her sense of well-being in this phase of her life and to her ability to relate deeply to others she encounters.

Mortality and Spirituality

Several people connected a growing awareness of their mortality with their spiritual orientation. From their perspective, mortality is an inherently spiritual matter requiring spiritual insight. Retired corporate executive John finds that this awareness of his mortality has created in him an increased interest in spiritual topics. One manifestation of this change is his attitude toward Sunday sermons given by the pastor of his church. Earlier in life he often resented or tuned out sermons that dealt personally and practically with spiritual topics. Now, not being challenged on this level disappoints him.

Rodney, another retired executive, expressed a different sentiment. In his words, "I have spent a lot of time distinguishing myself in the eyes of other people. Now I need to be more attuned to distinguishing myself in the eyes of God." Rodney experienced a spiritual transformation, resulting in a more internalized sense of authority. He began looking less to others and more to God.

Mark, a retired pastor, has found that reflecting on his mortality brings both the strengths and weaknesses of his relationship to God into sharper focus. He feels that certain areas of this relationship still need to be made right, and doing this is a priority for him at this stage of life.

Sharing Feelings about Mortality with Others

Some who experienced a growing sense of their own mortality were comfortable sharing these feelings with others, and some were not. Ted, mentioned above, has become comfortable speaking about his own mortality with those closest to him. Mark, on the other hand, finds it difficult to talk about the topic with anyone else. He has not yet expressed his thoughts to even those closest to him, though he feels he needs to do so.

Expressing such deep feelings can be hard for anyone, but it may pose a particular problem for pastors and priests who believe they should have matters of mortality all figured out. Or, in the words of one pastor, "Those of us who have been responsible for dealing with grace may have difficulty in fully experiencing it ourselves." This is only one of a number of areas where retired pastors and priests face challenges unique to them. (Another example noted by some clergy, discussed more fully in chapter 3, was the need to separate themselves from the congregation they had served immediately upon retirement so as not to interfere with the work of their successor.)

Our own frequent or serious illness and the death of contemporaries can push us to come to grips with our own mortality. The experiences described in this chapter suggest, however, that meeting this challenge can serve as an important catalyst for spiritual and personal growth in our retirement years. Choosing to live in today's opportunities rather than tomorrow's obligations can reduce our feelings of anxiety while allowing us to be fully present to those we encounter. It can also motivate us to give more serious attention to spiritual realities. And we may come to the point of being able to share our feelings about this highly personal topic with those close to us.

Questions for Reflection

1. The authors suggest that we more easily accept taxes than we do death. Do you agree or disagree? Why is death a topic we tend to avoid in our society?

2. What events earlier in your life have caused you to come face-to-face with your mortality? What was this like for you? How has that realization continued to impact your life?

3. Confronting death's reality can be beneficial. To the extent you have thought about your own mortality, how has that process brought insight or clarity to you?

4. What practical steps do you still need to take for the benefit of those you will leave behind when you die?

CHAPTER

10

Looking to the Future with Hope

THE RETIRED PROFESSIONALS we interviewed are in the earlier stages of retirement; their physical capabilities are either close to those of the preretirement years or else reduced mobility or other physical limitation is modest enough that they continue to live independently. Their insights have allowed us to draw conclusions primarily about preretirement and these first two stages of retirement life identified in the Introduction. But for most, retirement moves into a phase where daily living requires the assistance of others. This chapter offers insights about this final stage of retirement, which is also the final stage of life. The content of this chapter is based on conversations with people who work with retired persons and the insights of the authors, one of whom (Jerry) served as pastor for several congregations with a large number of retired individuals.

LOOKING PAST EIGHTY

As Paula moved into her late seventies, she sensed that she needed to adapt to her diminishing physical and mental capacities. A person of strong faith, she acknowledged letting go as an essential spiritual discipline, especially as one ages. She often joked about her own strong will and understood the challenge of giving up ego attachments (those things that have given her a sense of self-worth and independence). After a minor car accident, she relinquished her driver's license. Later, she confessed it was one of the hardest things she had ever done. After a couple of falls, she checked herself into a retirement facility. Neither decision was made for her by others; both came from within herself as she reflected on where she was being led in her life. In both cases she experienced doubt and depression, sometimes for months, and in both cases she worked through her feelings to the point of acceptance and even to peace and joy.

Paula is exceptional. Individuals seldom make these adjustments without outside intervention. As we age, we tend to resist change in routine. We want things to stay the same, but they don't.

Paula's spirituality provides an ongoing source of strength for her. She sees the ego as the source of willpower but not as the ultimate source of identity. As a Christian, she believes her true self is "hidden with Christ" (Col. 3:3). She believes that the quest for this true self becomes clearer when the ego diminishes. She sees her post-eighty years as her final formation as a Christ-follower. In dying, she believes she will be going home.

Role Models

As a person of faith, Paula serves as a role model for others—one of the most loving, joyful persons you will ever meet. She feels the pain of her losses acutely, and yet she moves on to embrace an entirely hopeful perspective. Her many friends and family love being with her, and she loves being with them. She extends her full presence to them, not dwelling on the past or anxiously worrying about the future. She harbors no naïvete about the distortions and selfishness of our modern world; she simply focuses more on goodness than evil.

At age fifty or sixty or seventy, we may think no role models exist. Paula and others like her refute that idea. In early retirement we do well to look for someone to inspire our own journey.

Many candidates present themselves, but we have to make the effort to notice them. A retired businessman and his wife, still active in their nineties, communicate their sense of closeness to each other and their love for life. After sixty years, their marriage is still a source of inspiration for many. An engineer discovers that in his retirement he has time to communicate compassion for others and spends hours of volunteer time visiting men with HIV/AIDS. A devoted husband grieves the death of his wife and is forced by physical limitations to move to a nursing home where he is restricted to a wheelchair. The physical limitations do not limit his sense of humor or purpose; he gives joy and finds it by talking and joking with the care-center attendants and other residents. If you look for inspiration in those who are older than you when you retire, you will find it.

DEPRESSION, COUNSELING, AND MEDICATION

As in the general population, depression is not uncommon in older people. Fortunately, the more we learn about depression the less stigma is attached to psychotherapeutic counseling. Antidepressants, when prescribed by a knowledgeable physician, can play a big part in treatment. While attitude and faith are strong factors in resolving despair, people with strong religious sensitivities are not immune to psychological problems. Paula, mentioned earlier in this chapter, sought to regain a positive attitude through prayer and contemplation as she coped with her losses. She also sought counseling and medication to help her through the most demanding periods in her adjustment. Medical and psychological methods, when used wisely, can complement rather than compete with a healthy spiritual life.

Regular medical checkups and open, honest conversations about psychological well-being are essential to good mental health. We need not overlook the importance of supportive friendships and family relationships during difficult transitions. And physical exercise and good nutrition are powerful antidotes in dealing with depression. As we age, we may moderate our exercise program, but it doesn't become any less necessary. Physical, spiritual, and psychological factors are intimately related.

ANOTHER RELOCATION

When we settle into our retirement home, we may think our moving days are over. In fact, our home at age sixty-five may not meet our needs when we are eighty.

One person in our survey decided to enter a graduated-care facility immediately upon retirement rather than wait until later. Rachel gave leadership to an extensive ministry of her diocese prior to her retirement. She has now been in her new home for about a year and remains pleased with her decision to move there "while still able to contribute and get involved." She finds many aspects of this living arrangement fulfilling: she enjoys helping the older residents; she gives her time as a member of the board of the facility; she has more free time to give to her family; and she works on her "secret dreams"—hobbies and vocational interests she never had time to pursue before.

Rachel's decision to enter this facility immediately after retirement is unusual. Often, people avoid relocating after retirement until they have to. The first ten or fifteen years of retirement can be quite freeing. Without work restraints and with fewer family obligations, many discover that these are the best years of their lives. It is hard to give up this freedom and face the reality of declining health. Moving to a graduated-care facility, a senior apartment, or an assisted living facility can be a hard decision. Family members often influence the decision. It is not always easy to navigate role reversals as an adult child or a nephew or niece assumes authority for a move or a placement. Who wants to be told by a loved one that it is time to sell their home?

While relocating may be difficult, doing so before a crisis occurs may be wise. Both timing and good options can make this decision easier. One factor to consider: it's usually easier to make new friends when you are seventy-five than eighty-five.

Aging adults today have more services available to them. Home health care, geriatric social workers, advocacy groups, and networking provide good alternatives. Talking to friends, checking with a trusted doctor or pastor, searching the Internet, and calling agencies and services in your area may reveal even more options.

A DYNAMIC PROCESS: FRIENDSHIPS AND PLANNING

The final stage of retirement—the final stage of life—is dynamic, just like the rest of life. People in their eighties and nineties continue to experience the dynamic process of relationships, perhaps in a new way. Because in later life we tend to drop pretense in favor of honesty, elders can become sought-after companions by people of all ages.

Retirees reflect on their past and seek to integrate wisdom gleaned from a lifetime of experience. As the legacy of our lives becomes clearer, we often tell family history and autobiographical stories more accurately. As we enter this final stage of retirement, we make other adjustments as well. Estate plans made earlier are adjusted to reflect more accurately the values we wish to embrace. Funeral and memorial plans are laid out, not as morbid activity but because we want to pass on certain aspects of ourselves, our values, and preferences. These later years are critical to shaping our legacy.

QUESTIONS FOR REFLECTION

1. The authors describe a woman who has lived her later life as a role model for others. Whom do you know who has exhibited such grace and peace in his or her later years that you would seek to emulate in this phase of life?

2. What do you see as the main issues and emotions around giving up your driver's license? What steps might you take in advance to mitigate the effects of this change?

3. Even if you are currently far from the time of needing assistance in living, what steps might you take now to prepare for this eventuality? What do you think of Rachel's choice to enter a graduated-care facility while still in good health?

ADVICE

11

Advice to Preretirees

We have identified some of the key personal transitions, opportunities, and challenges encountered as people move from a full-time career to retirement. Implicit in each of the themes described in these chapters are steps that could be considered when planning for retirement. In this chapter we offer advice and questions for those looking forward to retirement and those who are in the early months of this life phase. These suggestions are drawn from the insights shared in the earlier chapters, our own personal experiences, and interview responses to the question: "If you had a younger friend contemplating or approaching retirement, what advice would you give him or her?" The recommendations fall into broad categories, including when and how to retire, developing a positive attitude toward this phase of life, and suggestions for the period immediately following retirement.

When and How to Retire

Several interviewees stressed the importance of deciding whether to continue practicing their profession in retirement or not. The value of making a decision about this issue was affirmed both by those who are and are not doing something in retirement related to their former profession. Jeffrey, a retired business executive, said that the key question to ask is whether or not you really enjoy your work. If the answer is an unqualified yes, then consider continuing to work full-time or explore a part-time option that allows you to pursue some of the enjoyable facets of your profession.

Thomas, who loves the pastoral ministry and has continued in this role on a part-time basis in his early years of retirement, expressed a cautionary comment about a part-time option: establish at the outset the boundaries of work time. Otherwise, either our own work habits or others' expectations will cause us to move toward a full-time responsibility for part-time pay. Thomas points out that no one is well served by allowing a drift back into full-time work, not the semiretiree, not the employer, nor individuals being served by the efforts of the semiretired person.

So when might we fully retire? George, a retired faculty member, suggested that the ideal time presents itself when work impedes our desire to follow our true interests or passions. This assumption presupposes that we know ourselves well enough to know our deepest interests. In fact, moving to this level of self-knowledge becomes a priority when preparing for retirement.

As several men and women pointed out, we do not always choose the timing of our retirement. Among those we interviewed, the time of retirement was sometimes determined by corporate mergers or policies, declining health, or other circumstances beyond their control. And some continue to work part-time to supplement retirement income or savings. Neither financial position nor the reason for retiring at a particular time seemed to affect the essential nature of the transitions, opportunities, and challenges faced by these individuals. Rather, as Judy, a retired professional from a nonprofit organization indicated, it is important to accept even circumstances beyond our control with a positive attitude and move on.

FINANCES

Although our interviews and discussions focused on emotional and spiritual dimensions of retirement, several people advised developing a realistic view of one's financial situation in this phase of life. As Ron, another retired business executive pointed out, this allows retirees to determine the "financial envelope in which to live." Ron further shared his view and experience that, if married, *both* spouses need a good understanding of their financial picture. Having a clear financial picture resulted in some individuals being more generous than they had anticipated, some deciding to live more modestly than before, some continuing to work part-time, and some downsizing to free up money to pursue a hobby or interest. We have encountered individuals in all of these financial circumstances who live fulfilling lives in retirement; finances alone do not determine fulfillment. Fulfillment comes when we understand our situation clearly and move into it with anticipation, planning, and wisdom.

EXPLORATION OF INTERESTS

Retirement can allow us to pursue interests and passions that we had neither the time nor the freedom to explore earlier. Some of us may already have a list of interests we are eager to try out. Others may need some time to research options before finding an activity to pursue. While the best approach to discovering our interests may differ, we heard a few commonsense suggestions for all.

One idea: use the years leading up to retirement to experiment with areas of potential interest. That is what Ann, an author who started writing as she approached retirement, did. She prepared for a fulfilling retirement by getting to know herself and then trying out an activity that she believed she would enjoy in her later years.

Another way to find our passion is to volunteer part-time in an area that we might wish to devote ourselves more fully in retirement. Such modest expenditures of time offer potential richness to our preretirement life and indicate how we want to invest ourselves after we retire. We may also be well served by thinking back over our adulthood and listing those things that we found interesting but for one reason or another could not pursue at the time. Are they of sufficient interest now to be revisited? And finally, it may help to talk over options with a family member or friend who knows us well and can offer another perspective. Through this type of exploration and preparation, the smaller world of retirement may turn out to be a richer world of new opportunities for personal growth and service to others.

EXPECTATIONS OF KEY RELATIONSHIPS

The married retirees we spoke with often mentioned a common concern: that spousal expectations of retirement did not always match. Before retirement, couples may need to address not only financial issues but also the vision each has of retirement. This includes practical matters as how much time will be spent together and apart, what activities will be pursued together and independently, the aspirations and dreams of each for this phase of life, and areas of fear or uncertainty. It may help to think through some what-ifs. For example, what if one of us develops a condition that requires a high degree of care? What preparations do we need to make so that life will be as uncomplicated as possible for the surviving spouse in the likely event that one of us predeceases the other? Such conversations need to take place sooner rather than later. And depending on family situation (married or single, children or not), other family relationships or friendships may also merit such clear communication before retirement.

FRIENDSHIPS

Friendships are so crucial to a fulfilling retirement that time invested in deepening key relationships and in developing approaches to making new friends before retirement will serve us well in this later phase of life. In our interviews and conversations, people stressed the importance of long-term friendships sustained through mutual effort and, in some cases, even sacrifice. In almost every case, these friendships originated during the work or school years. So we need to ask ourselves long before retirement, "What am I doing, or what do I need to do to foster such continuing relationships?" Whether or not we relocate when we retire, we will also need to make new friends in this phase of life. We may want to think carefully about how we make friends beyond the work environment before retirement and how we might be more intentional about this in preparation for life beyond work.

Relocation

We have noted some of the difficulties and disillusionment that can accompany relocation to a new community in retirement and that this adjustment may be facilitated by choosing a relatively new community or neighborhood. Even though this transition may have difficulties, it is often warranted by other considerations. One of the coauthors of this book (Jack) and his wife relocated in retirement to be closer to grandchildren, allowing them to invest more fully in these relationships during this phase of life. When the other coauthor (Jerry) and his wife retire, they plan to return to a community where they lived at an earlier time in their careers.

We suggest that relocation options be thoroughly explored and advantages and disadvantages carefully considered before taking the plunge. If considering a move to a community where you have not previously resided, it may be wise to spend some sustained time there to see how it fits, perhaps during a vacation or other break in the normal work routine. Moreover, visits at different times of the year can inform assessment of the climate and culture of the community. Talking with other people who have retired to this community can help, along with the availability of opportunities or activities you consider important.

Attitude

Tim, a retired leader in a major Protestant denomination, spoke with clarity about "leaning into this phase of life with a sense of expectancy." Several of the people interviewed displayed this attitude, embarking upon retirement as yet another adventure or challenge. And the retirees we have interacted with give ample evidence of the richness of experience in this phase of life. It can be a time of unique personal growth and creativity as well as service to others. But Tim put his finger on the key requirement to experiencing this kind of retirement: an attitude of expectancy and adventure.

What might get in the way of our approaching retirement with such a sense of expectancy? One possibility is the fear associated with moving from the known to the unknown. What will my financial situation be like when I no longer have a work income? How will I spend all that time? How will I face the reality of declining physical capabilities and my own mortality? Meet such fears head-on by discussing them with a trusted relative or friend. In William P. Young's best-selling novel *The Shack*, Jesus says, "The darkness hides the true size of fears and lies and regrets. . . . The truth is they are more shadow than reality, so they seem bigger in the dark. When the light shines into the places they live inside you, you start to see them for what they are."[1] Voicing some of these fears or uncertainties can shine light on them, and you can see them for what they are.

A Plan

Several individuals pointed out the importance of having developed a plan for retirement. Even though these plans may be only partly worked out at retirement, they still form a springboard for moving forward. Perhaps as important to the retirees as the need for a plan were the practical steps for arriving at such a plan. Two recommendations carry a lot of weight: (1) Spend time with retired individuals to learn what has worked for them and why. (2) Spend time with one or more trusted friends, talking through the choices. You might pursue this latter option one-on-one or in a small-group study. Another alternative resembles a Quaker Clearness Committee, a small group of mature individuals who hear you out and ask clarifying questions.[2] One of the coauthors (Jack) and his wife met with such a group when deciding whether to accept a temporary academic position in another part of the world or to move closer to their grandchildren when they retired. The purpose is not so much to solicit advice as to articulate thoughts to others who listen carefully and raise questions when we seem not to have formulated a clear direction.

When We Finally Reach Retirement

Our interviews yielded a few practical suggestions for new retirees. Jim, a retired physician, said he allowed a few months to adjust to retirement before making any big changes or undertaking any new responsibilities. Not all shared his perspective, though, and some people moved or took on new responsibilities fairly quickly. June, a retired pastor, found it helpful in the early days of retirement to have a daily and weekly schedule. She and many others we spoke with found themselves at loose ends with no structure or schedule in this initial period. And Rachel, a retired professor, spoke for many when she noted the importance in the early days of exploring areas of potential interest and service. Finally, Tammy, a retired nurse, mentioned finding ways quickly to grow intellectually, spiritually, physically, and relationally. She particularly emphasized the need to meet and interact with a wide range of people, including those of other ages.

Questions for Reflection

1. The authors offer advice to those approaching and in the early stages of retirement. What advice would you offer based on your experiences or others you know who are retired?

2. If you are retired now, what might you have done differently as you approached retirement or lived out the early stages of retirement?

3. Several people we interviewed noted how different their retirement experience has been than its portrayal by the popular media as a carefree time invested in leisure activities that satisfy desires or aspirations. In what ways do you want or expect your retirement to differ from such portrayals?

4. Retired or not, what choices or decisions do you face now with regard to your future? What steps might help you weigh your options as you think these matters through?

5. What is one of your fears about the future? How does the quote from *The Shack* address this fear: "The darkness hides the true size of fears and lies and regrets. . . . The truth is they are more shadow than reality, so they seem bigger in the dark. When the light shines into the places they live inside you, you start to see them for what they are"?

CHAPTER

12

What Organizations Could Do Better

The personal dimensions of retirement pose critical questions for those approaching and in retirement. They also suggest challenges and opportunities for organizations and individuals who serve the preretiree and retiree population, as well as for those who try to recruit from this population for volunteer or paid positions. The former group includes employers, financial advisers, lifelong learning programs of colleges and universities, and churches and other community groups with significant retiree and preretiree populations. The latter is made up of the broad array of organizations that depend on volunteers (or in some cases paid retirees) to fulfill their organization's objectives. The key question posed for those who provide a service to preretirees and retirees is how to assist their clientele in appreciating, preparing for, and navigating the personal dimensions of the transition from full-time employment to whatever follows. And for organizations that wish to recruit retirees, how might they best draw upon the gifts, experiences, and interests of these individuals in meaningful ways?

EMPLOYERS

Employers often provide a variety of services to their employees as they approach retirement. Information and seminars on retiree pension and health insurance benefits, Social Security, and Medicare are among these services. Receiving accurate information on these and related topics is critical. We suggest that employers also consider highlighting the personal dimensions of retirement. One approach would be to distribute a resource such as this book to employees one or two years prior to their planned retirement. Then as part of the preretirement seminar or seminar series, a human resource professional summarizes the topic, followed by a panel discussion involving carefully selected, recent retirees from the organization who are willing to share their own experiences.

FINANCIAL ADVISERS

Many people work with a financial adviser, particularly in the later stages of their professional life as they become more conscious of the financial resources that retirement may require. Both financial planners and retirees we have spoken with suggest that the personal challenges and opportunities associated with transition from full-time employment should shape one's financial plan. Or as Jeff, a financial adviser, explained, "It is helpful for a couple or individual that I am assisting to know what they are planning for." Given the long-term relationship of trust that financial planners have with their clients and the importance of the financial plan serving the retirement aspirations of these clients, we suggest that financial advisers consider providing information on the personal dimensions of retirement to clients a few years before the projected retirement date. The suggestion might also be made for couples to talk through these personal dimensions of retirement and come to agreement as a basis for their financial plan.

UNIVERSITIES AND COLLEGES

Because the years following full-time employment can be a time of great intellectual growth, many colleges and universities are attempting to involve retirees in their institutions. Some have formal lifelong learning institutes, such as those established under the auspices of the Osher Foundation (now at over 120 colleges and universities in the United States).[1] Others provide opportunities to audit classes at no cost or at a reasonable cost. Whatever the specifics, many colleges and universities have programs in place to serve older adults. The benefits to the participants include both intellectual growth and an opportunity to make new friends. The institution of higher learning benefits because the initiative contributes to its community and also develops an additional constituency and support base in the community. Another benefit derives from the intergenerational character of the program. Academic departments can tap older adults in these programs as research subjects or panel discussion participants, and their presence helps younger adults see the value of learning as a lifelong endeavor.

Those programs that already reach a large number of older students might consider another step. Many organizations depend on volunteers for critical functions. The Osher Lifelong Learning Institute at Furman University is typical in this respect. It currently serves approximately one thousand students in an academic year, offering about ninety courses per term. Some 250 volunteers play central roles in the organization, serving as officers, committee members, faculty members, and in other positions. Such organizations might consider interviewing new students to ascertain how their interests and expertise would fit with available volunteer opportunities in the organization, perhaps using some of the recruiting techniques described below.

ORGANIZATIONS SEEKING TO RECRUIT RETIREES

Retired professionals represent a tremendous resource, both for our society at large and for local and national organizations that carry out their missions through volunteers. Some authors have argued that individuals in the coming wave of baby boomer retirees have the potential to make major contributions to our society, as "our only increasing natural resource."[2] Yet, no institution appears to draw upon this resource effectively on a large scale. Organizations have traditionally looked to older adults to fulfill routine responsibilities that require little expertise, training, oversight, or screening. Such roles are important and need to be filled, but they rarely tap into what highly skilled persons with a lifetime of professional expertise and experience can offer. Another author points to some of the challenges of tapping into this potential, perhaps the most formidable being getting to know prospective volunteers and their skills and designing positions that make use of these skills and interests.[3] Often an organization does not have staff with the time or training to do this.

Organizations interested in recruiting highly capable preretirees and retirees might select and train a group of individuals (volunteers themselves) to interview potential volunteers to discover their areas of expertise, experience, and interest. Organizations might accomplish this goal by adapting the questionnaire and interview process we employed in researching this book (see Appendix B, page 109). The organization would provide basic training in interviewing, and the results could then be reviewed by the staff to match potential volunteers with areas of interest. This information also can be used to structure meaningful programs of recognition of these volunteers for their contributions to the organization.

FAITH COMMUNITIES, OTHER ORGANIZATIONS

The individuals we interviewed agree that churches, synagogues, and other community organizations can assist preretirees and retirees in addressing the personal challenges of this phase of life. Religious organizations seem particularly well suited to this because of their emphasis on the personal and relational dimensions of life and because in many communities they serve a significant number of preretirees and retirees. Below we have indicated a few ideas for engaging older adults with the understanding that some might better be carried out by churches or synagogues and some by other community organizations.

Preretirement and Early Retirement Seminars, Workshops, and Classes

Joe, a retired business executive, says retirement is like getting married—it is a major adjustment that cannot be fully appreciated until you are there. But he took the analogy further, pointing out that couples approaching marriage are often helped in the transition by thinking through important questions before the wedding. He suggested, as others did, that seminars, workshops, or classes could be valuable for individuals approaching and in early stages of retirement. These instructional venues provide an environment in which the relational, self-image, and spiritual dimensions of retirement can be explored in a variety of ways.

Organizing these offerings could be as simple as having a group read this book or other resources and discuss the questions raised by the material. A one-day event such as a seminar or workshop has the advantage of bringing together people who might be reluctant to join a smaller group. Offering this ministry communicates to the congregation and community that the church or synagogue recognizes the importance of this transition and opens the way for emerging lay leadership to offer ongoing ministry to this population.

Small Groups

We were struck by the positive impact that sustained participation in small groups had on the lives of retirees. In today's mobile society vast distances often separate individuals from other parts of their families; their long-term participation in a small group provides friendship and support in the years prior to and following retirement. Judy, a retired business owner, described a Bible study and fellowship group that she and her husband have been attending for over a decade. When it started, all the group members still worked outside the home; now several of the participants have retired. This group has helped its individual participants in times of illness, loss of spouse, and other difficulties. Their deep investment in one another's lives creates community in the best sense. Of course, a functioning small group meets these needs for people of any age, but it has the potential to provide a much-needed support base for retirees.

Topics related to retirement may be introduced to an ongoing small group. Or a small group could organize around issues related to retirement for short-term or long-term study.

Intergenerational Mentoring Opportunities

A number of retirees involved in churches mentioned that they mentor younger people. Examples ranged from tutoring children, to "adopting" a college student from a local college, to encouraging younger men or women who are trying to live out their faith with the pressures of family and career life. Such mentoring relationships not only benefited the person being mentored; they also deeply satisfied the retirees.

Caring for the Caregivers

Because older adults often have caregiving responsibilities for loved ones, churches and synagogues may want to consider developing support systems for them. Support can come in many forms: friendly visitation, respite care, day programs for socialization, Stephen Ministry, volunteers who do cleaning or repairing, shepherding programs, and phone trees.

Confidential Counseling

A number of retirees pointed out that confidential counseling from a currently active counselor or from a qualified retiree could be helpful. Such areas as finances, addiction, grief, loneliness, and depression all warranted attention. Some organizations, for example, might have a qualified, retired financial planner or other professional who could give financial advice on a volunteer basis or provide substance-abuse counseling for retirees in recovery.

Matching Passion with Need

A key for all organizations that work with volunteers is to find ways to match the volunteers' interests and passions with the needs of the community. Paying careful attention to a potential volunteer's life interests helps organizations place volunteers in meaningful positions. Religious organizations need to have an up-to-date list of volunteer opportunities. A central clearinghouse that posts opportunities on a Web site, for example, would be a valuable investment for many denominations.

A Unique Role

One service to preretirees and retirees that organizations with a religious orientation can provide is meaningful discussion of the inherently spiritual dimensions of life. Most obvious is coming to terms with the reality of our mortality, but other areas merit discussion. Meeting the reality of declining physical capabilities, as well as developing a self-image rooted in personal beliefs, relationships, or service to others (rather than in performance) can be inherently spiritual matters. Religious organizations can play a valuable role in providing a framework of meaning for this phase of life.

Questions for Reflection

1. The authors offer several suggestions for organizations seeking to serve retirees and those approaching retirement. From your own experience which of these suggestions seem important? What others would you add?

2. Retired professionals may find a match between their interests and capabilities and the needs and expectations of churches and other volunteer organizations a hard one. What has been your experience? What steps might organizations take to tap more fully into the resource represented by the talents and experiences of the retiree population?

3. What opportunities might there be in your community for you to be a mentor?

NOTES

INTRODUCTION, RETIREMENT: THE PERSONAL SIDE

1. Gail Sheehy, *New Passages: Mapping Your Life across Time* (New York: Random House, 1995).
2. Kathy Charmaz, *Constructing Grounded Theory: A Practical Guide through Qualitative Analysis* (Thousand Oaks, CA: Sage Publications, 2006), 25–35.
3. Richard H. Gentzler Jr., *The Graying of the Church: A Leader's Guide for Older-Adult Ministries in The United Methodist Church* (Nashville, TN: Discipleship Resources, 2004).
4. For example, the seminal work of Daniel J. Levinson's *Seasons of a Man's Life* (New York: Ballantine Books, 1978) is based on interviews of forty men. The better-known expansion of this work on all of the "passages" or transitions of adult life—Gail Sheehy's *Passages: Predictable Crises of Adult Life* (New York: Ballantine Books, 2006)—involved 115 life histories. The number of interviews we conducted exceeded the saturation criterion often used in qualitative social science research, which means that we conducted enough interviews that we were hearing the same themes and subthemes.

CHAPTER 2: NAVIGATING FAMILY RELATIONSHIPS

1. Lillian S. Hawthorne, *Sisters and Brothers All These Years: Taking Another Look at the Longest Relationship in Your Life* (Acton, MA: VanderWyk and Burnham, 2003), 53.

CHAPTER 3: VALUING FRIENDSHIPS

1. Benjamin Cornwell, Edward O. Laumann, and L. Philip Schumm, "The Social Connectedness of Older Adults: A National Profile," *American Sociological Review* 73, no. 2 (April 2008): 185–203.
2. Glenn Ruffenach and Kelly Greene, "Home and Family: Beyond the Nest Egg: What to Ask Yourself about Retirement; Key Questions Include: Go to Work or Not? Relocate or Stay Put?" *Wall Street Journal* (June 7, 2007): D2.

CHAPTER 4: RETIRING *to* AS WELL AS *from* SOMETHING

1. Greg Mortenson and David Oliver Relin, *Three Cups of Tea: One Man's Mission to Promote Peace . . . One School at a Time* (New York: Viking Penguin, 2006).
2. Marc Freedman, *Prime Time: How Baby Boomers Will Revolutionize Retirement and Transform America* (New York: PublicAffairs,1999), 83. The

author offers a more detailed account of the National Service Corps and other initiatives that draw upon the experience and maturity of retirees.

CHAPTER 5: GROWING SPIRITUALLY AND INTELLECTUALLY

1. K. Warner Schaie, Neal M. Krause, and Alan Booth, eds., *Religious Influences on the Health and Well-Being in the Elderly* (New York: Springer Publishing, 2004).
2. James A. Autry, *The Spirit of Retirement: Creating a Life of Meaning and Personal Growth* (Roseville, CA: Prima Publishing/Random House, 2002).
3. Harold G. Koenig, *Purpose and Power in Retirement: New Opportunities for Meaning and Significance* (Philadelphia: Templeton Foundation Press, 2002).
4. Richard H. Gentzler Jr. and Craig Kennet Miller, *Forty-Sixty: A Study for Midlife Adults Who Want to Make a Difference* (Nashville, TN: Discipleship Resources, 2003).
5. Freedman, *Prime Time*, 23–24.
6. Henri J. M. Nouwen, *Can You Drink the Cup?* (Notre Dame, IN: Ave Maria Press, 1996), 26.

CHAPTER 7: WHO AM I NOW THAT I'M RETIRED?

1. Joan Chittister, *The Gift of Years: Growing Older Gracefully* (New York: BlueBridge/United Tribes Media, 2008), 107.
2. Richard L. Morgan, *Remembering Your Story: Creating Your Own Spiritual Autobiography* (Nashville, TN: Upper Room Books, 2002).
3. Chittister, *The Gift of Years*, 5.

CHAPTER 11: ADVICE TO PRERETIREES

1. William P. Young, *The Shack* (Los Angeles: Windblown Media, 2007), 174–75.
2. For a description of the Clearness Committee process, see Stephen V. Doughty with Marjorie J. Thompson, *The Way of Discernment*, Participant's Book (Nashville, TN: Upper Room Books, 2008), 82.

CHAPTER 12: WHAT ORGANIZATIONS COULD DO BETTER

1. Osher Lifelong Learning Institutes, http://www.osherfoundation. org/index.php?olli
2. Freedman, *Prime Time*, 16.
3. Jennifer C. Berkshire, "Tapping Older Volunteers," *Chronicle of Philanthropy* (2005). http://philanthropy.com/free/articles/v17/ i17/17004201.htm

Appendix A

Resources for Individual and Group Study

This book is intended for both individual and group use: for those approaching and in retirement and those seeking to serve retirees. So, each chapter closes with questions for personal and group reflection. Here we highlight other resources that may be useful to consider for individuals or groups.

Books

Richard H. Gentzler Jr. and Craig Kennet Miller, *Forty-Sixty: A Study for Midlife Adults Who Want to Make a Difference* (Nashville, TN: Discipleship Resources, 2003).

This resource is for individuals in their forties through their sixties who want to make a difference in this phase of life. It deals with some of the personal realities of growing through midlife (changing relationships with children, grandchildren, and parents; thoughts on making a real contribution in this phase of life; and spiritual development). Each chapter contains a scripture meditation and questions for group reflection.

Richard H. Gentzler Jr., *Aging and Ministry in the 21st Century: An Inquiry Approach* (Nashville, TN: Discipleship Resources, 2008).

This book addresses topics such as retirement, spirituality, caregiving, and mortality within the context of churches and other religious organizations serving older adults.

Marc Freedman, *Prime Time: How Baby Boomers Will Revolutionize Retirement and Transform America* (New York: PublicAffairs, 1999).

The author argues persuasively that retirees, if mobilized, can have a major impact on society. *Prime Time* provides good background on past efforts and proposals to do this, as well as personal stories of retirees who have made a difference through their own volunteer or other efforts.

Bob Buford, *Halftime: Changing Your Game Plan from Success to Significance* (Grand Rapids, MI: Zondervan, 2009).

This book also considers the transitions that occur in the middle years, and, like *Forty-Sixty*, is written from a Christian perspective. It focuses on moving from achieving success to realizing significance. This book has a variety of resources available (for example, a study guide and video). Visit the Web site for the Halftime Network at http://www.halftime.org

James A. Autry, *The Spirit of Retirement: Creating a Life of Meaning and Personal Growth* (Roseville, CA: Prima Publishing/Random House, 2002).

This book deals with the spiritual dimension of retirement, specifically with personal facets of the transition to retirement as well as with areas of personal growth and contribution that can be realized in this phase of life. These include growth in relationships, contribution, and spirituality.

Richard N. Bolles and John E. Nelson, *What Color Is Your Parachute? for Retirement: Planning Now for the Life You Want* (Berkeley, CA: Ten Speed Press, 2007).

While most of the literature on retirement deals with aspects of finances, health, and location, a few books and articles representing a broader view have appeared. *What Color Is Your Parachute? for Retirement* provides a conceptual model for retirement that focuses on meaning and engagement as well as pleasure as part of personal fulfillment. It treats finances, health, and personal satisfaction as integrated parts of ideal retirement. It also offers practical exercises to help readers come to grips with the key elements of their hoped-for retirement.

Joan Chittister, *The Gift of Years: Growing Older Gracefully* (New York: BlueBridge/United Tribes Media, 2008).

The Gift of Years identifies forty life themes related to aging. Chittister begins each chapter with a quotation (from a wide range of sources) and ends each chapter by identifying both a "burden" and a "blessing." Her book challenges the underlying attitudes of aging in American culture and encourages the reader to embrace the freedom and possibility of this time of life. Written for a general audience, this book could be used by individuals or in groups to reflect on the challenge of aging.

Stephen V. Doughty with Marjorie J. Thompson, *The Way of Discernment*, Participant's Book (Nashville, TN: Upper Room Books, 2008).

Marjorie J. Thompson, *The Way of Discernment*, Leader's Guide (Nashville, TN: Upper Room Books, 2008).

As part of the Companions in Christ series, this small-group resource can help the person entering retirement who seeks to discern God's call for this phase of life. The Participant's Book explores the meaning of discernment and its challenges. The Leader's Guide will guide the convener in shepherding the group through its ten-week journey.

Allan B. Chinen, *In the Ever After: Fairy Tales and the Second Half of Life* (Wilmette, IL: Chiron Publications, 1989).

Psychiatrist Allan Chinen offers Jungian insights into a collection of fairy tales from around the world. This book invites readers to look below the surface of the narrative to discover deeper truths. A fascinating look at aging from a cross-cultural ancient/modern perspective.

Joseph F. Miraglia, *Fit or Misfit: The Successful Executive Attempts To Serve the Church* (2008). Unpublished manuscript available from the author at Joemiraglia@msn.com.

Joe Miraglia, a retired corporate executive, relates his experiences of working with other corporate executives and pastors to utilize the capabilities of executives in the church environment. He identifies mismatches in expectations and cultures that can get in the way of retired executives finding meaningful roles in religious institutions. This would be helpful reading for retired professionals seeking to make their way in the church setting and for church leadership seeking to serve populations of retired professionals.

Lillian S. Hawthorne, *Sisters and Brothers All These Years: Taking Another Look at the Longest Relationship in Your Life* (Acton, MA: VanderWyk and Burnham, 2003).

This book focuses on how sibling relationships develop later in life. The majority of adults in the United States (as high as 80 percent) have siblings, and these relationships are unique in that they generally span both our childhood and adult years. As the author notes, it is particularly important to focus on the dual responsibilities of "finding" siblings with whom we may have had limited contact through our earlier adult years and preparing to lose our siblings.

Peg Senturia, Stan Davis, Hy Kempler, Prudence King, and Rhoda Wald, eds., *New Pathways for Aging* (Cambridge, MA: Harvard Institute for Learning in Retirement, 2009).

This collection of essays and poems by twenty-seven participants in the Harvard Institute for Learning in Retirement are first-person accounts of accomplished individuals. The writing covers the themes of identity, learning, community, mortality, and more.

OTHER BOOKS ON TOPICS RELATED TO RETIREMENT

K. Warner Schaie, Neal M. Krause, and Alan Booth, eds., *Religious Influences on the Health and Well-Being in the Elderly* (New York: Springer Publishing, 2004).

This book offers insight into the relationship among religion, health, and well-being.

Christina M. Neill and Arnold S. Kahn, "The Role of Personal Spirituality and Religious Social Activity on the Life Satisfaction of Older Widowed Women," *Sex Roles: A Journal of Research* 40, nos. 3–4 (February 1999): 319–29.

This journal article explores the role of spirituality in life satisfaction for older, widowed women.

Yang Yang, "Social Inequalities in Happiness in the United States, 1972 to 2004: An Age-Period-Cohort Analysis," *American Sociological Review* 73, no. 2 (April 2008): 204–26.

Yang's research shows that the percentage of people who report being "very happy" actually increases with age after about age forty. This analysis takes into account such factors as gender, race, health, marital status, and educational level.

Benjamin Cornwell, Edward O. Laumann, and L. Philip Schumm, "The Social Connectedness of Older Adults: A National Profile," *American Sociological Review* 73, no. 2 (April 2008): 185–203.

This work shows that the average size of the social network of the oldest adults tends to be smaller than that of their younger counterparts, but the frequency of neighborly socializing, religious service attendance, and volunteering increases with age.

Daniel J. Levinson, *The Seasons of a Man's Life* (New York: Ballantine Books, 1978).

Levinson reports on some of the first modern research that supports the notion of stages of adult development.

Gail Sheehy, *New Passages: Mapping Your Life across Time* (New York: Random House, 1995).

Sheehy's original book, *Passages*, focused on stages of adult development up to age fifty. This later book focuses on the stages of development in what she refers to as "second adulthood," or ages forty-five to eighty-five and beyond.

Gail Sheehy, *Passages: Predictable Crises of Adult Life* (New York: Ballantine Books, 2006).

A thirtieth-anniversary edition of the original *Passages* volume.

Richard H. Gentzler Jr., *The Graying of the Church: A Leader's Guide for Older-Adult Ministry in The United Methodist Church* (Nashville, TN: Discipleship Resources, 2004).

This book addresses another fruitful area for individual as well as group study—adult life stages and transitions among these stages.

VIDEOS

Rueben P. Job, *Living Fully, Dying Well* (Nashville, TN: Abingdon Press, 2006).

This video-based study offers a way to facilitate reflection and conversation about the end of life. Organized around eight themes, the topics are addressed in a helpful manner by Job, several professionals, and laypeople.

Dewitt Jones, *For the Love of It* (St. Paul, MN: Star Thrower Distribution, 2007). www.fortheloveofitfilm.com.

This video features well-known photographer Dewitt Jones, whose work has appeared in *National Geographic* and in published collections of photographs. He addresses what it means to be passionate about a pursuit. The message about the importance of doing things that fill your life with energy is compelling and relevant to those approaching and early in retirement. Other materials, including a written transcript, a PowerPoint® summary, and a leader's guide, are also available.

PROGRAMS

The Academy for Spiritual Formation® (Upper Room Ministries/ General Board of Discipleship of the United Methodist Church). www.upperroom.org/academy Phone: 1-877-899-2781, ext. 7233.

The two-year Academy for Spiritual Formation is a retreat program for clergy and laity who strongly desire to grow in the Christian faith. Participants gather for five days every three months over a two-year period—a total of forty days on retreat. The Academy includes a balanced offering of worship, silence, instruction, and small-group sharing. Faculty present biblical, historical, and practical instruction; participants develop spiritual practices, read books, and create a ministry project. Ecumenically oriented, with participants and faculty from a wide variety of denominations, the Academy is accountable within the structures of the United Methodist Church through the General Board of Discipleship and Upper Room Ministries. This resource may be particularly helpful for persons entering retirement who are looking for a strong spiritual community in which to discern a ministry or direction for themselves. It is open to adults of all ages.

Appendix B

Interview Questionnaire

We used this questionnaire as the basis for the forty-five structured interviews that provided the foundation for this book.

Personal information

1. How long have you been retired?
2. How did you retire (close the door behind you, gradually, etc.)? Was the timing of your choosing?
3. What type of position did you have before retirement? How absorbed were you in your work?
4. How did you feel about retiring as the time approached?
5. Are there other significant life transitions that you experienced around this time (e.g., death of a loved one, moving to a new location, etc.)?
6. Now that you are retired, how are you spending your time?

Relationships

1. How has your retirement affected your family relationships (spouse, children, grandchildren, parents, siblings)?
2. How would you describe the impact of retirement on relationships outside your family, such as friends, neighbors, former coworkers, etc.?
3. What have you done to form new friendships/relationships since retirement?

Significance

1. In the years leading up to retirement, what were some of the key factors contributing to your sense of significance?

2. Now that you have retired, from where do you get your sense of significance?

SPIRITUALITY

1. Describe what spirituality looks like for you now.
2. What changes in your spiritual life have you experienced in the time leading up to and following retirement? Any real surprises?
3. What are some of your spiritual and emotional challenges at this point in life?
4. What are some personal qualities that you would like to develop during this stage of your life? What steps are you taking to realize these desires?
5. As you think of your own retirement experiences and challenges, what advice might you give to pastoral staffs or heads of ministries, things they might keep in mind as they serve a growing retiree population?
6. What advice might you give a person entering this phase of life?
7. What is your Myers-Briggs type?